Uncle John's

iFlush

Hurtling thru History

BATHROOM READER FOR KIDS ONLY!

by
Patrick
Merrell

NO LIVERWURST BEYOND THIS POINT

· ·

Bathroom Readers' Press
Ashland, Oregon

UNCLE JOHN'S IFLUSH: HURTLING THRU HISTORY
BATHROOM READER® FOR KIDS ONLY

For information, write:
The Bathroom Readers' Institute
P.O. Box 1117
Ashland, OR 97520
www.bathroomreader.com

Illustration and book design by Patrick Merrell
Dedicated to the Bronxville Library

ISBN-10: 1-60710-904-2 / ISBN-13: 978-1-60710-904-4

Library of Congress Cataloging-in-Publication Data
Uncle John's iflush hurtling thru history bathroom reader for kids only!
    pages cm
ISBN 978-1-60710-904-4 (hardback)
1. History--Anecdotes--Juvenile literature.
2. History--Miscellanea--Juvenile literature.
D10.U53 2013
909--dc23

2013014050

Printed in the United States of America
First Printing: July, 2013

17 16 15 14 13   6 5 4 3 2 1

Thanks: A hearty high-four (sorry, that's all the fingers
I have) to some humans who helped make this book possible:

Gordon Javna   Jay Newman   Blake Mitchum   Matt Lighty
Kim T. Griswell   Trina Janssen   Carly Stephenson   Brandon Walker
Brian Boone   Aaron Guzman   Joan Kyzer   Thomas Crapper

iOpener
Greetings

"History, shmistory!" That's what some people say. But not you. You know how exciting history can be. No? Well, that's because you haven't hurtled through history on an iFlush adventure!

As you'll soon see, history can be weird, amazing, and—hold on to your hairdo—fun! Here's a small sampling of what's in store:

- **U.S. Presidents:** Grover Cleveland's Rubber Jaw
- **World History:** Invasion of the Australian Bunnies
- **The Civil War:** Battleside Picnics
- **Ancient Egypt:** Mummy Cats
- **New York City:** World's Creepiest Island
- **Pacific Islands:** New Guinea's Treehouse Tribe, plus
- **History's Longest Year!**

So, whenever you're ready, go to the…

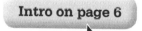

Intro on page 6

And we're off and flushing!

Contents

Bathroom user...

… prepare to dive into the greatest **toilet-themed adventure** ever devised by a group of **mad-scientist-type plumbers** and hosted by a bedraggled-yet-charming **lab rat** named **Dwayne**. That's me.

But, first, a quick explanation.

Copying how **computers** have been connected together to form the **Internet**, a top-secret plumbing team known as the **Four P's** linked the world's **sewer lines** together to create the **Interpipe**. You probably think I'm making that up, but this book is based on how it actually works!

The Four P's

Plumb Bob

Phyllis Tanks

P. Liddy

Portia Potty

Flush yourself down a toilet in **Walla Walla** (that's a city in the northwest part of the United States) and next thing you know, you're in **Katmandu** (that's like all the way on the other side of the world).

Wait, it gets even better!

The Four P's also created a waterproof device called the **iSwirl** that can be used to travel back in time, spinning through the years in a mere flush of the toilet! Is that not totally cool … and wet?

Yeah, I thought you'd agree.

So here's how this is going to work.

I'm gonna flush myself down this toilet, and you're gonna follow along. I'll be visiting a **different place** and a **different year** every time you turn the page. Solve the **puzzle** you find there, and you can move on— in one of three ways.

1. Follow the **pipes** to the next page; **2.** jump to the page shown on the **iSwirl** (in the lower right-hand corner)—the "**jump route**" will take you through the book in **chronological order** (from the earliest date to the most recent); or **3.** visit pages any old way you want!

Sound like a plan?

Then let's get going! I'll jump in, you turn the page, and we're on our way!

Note:

If you want to keep your book clean, use a separate piece of paper (toilet paper not recommended!) for solving the puzzles.

Go to the
page shown.

396 B.C. Welcome to the ancient **Olympic Games** held in the Greek city of **Olympia**. I've sneaked in for the final day of events, just in time for the four-horse **chariot race**. The **Spartans** have been waiting 24 years to win the event, and a princess named **Cynisca** might just be the one to pull it off.

Chariot Princess

The ancient Greeks loved their chariot races. But it cost a lot of money to put a winning team together: the chariot, horses, driver, and training. Only the very wealthy could afford it. Because of the danger involved, the owners rarely drove their chariots. However, they got the credit if their chariots won.

In 420 B.C., the Greek city-states of **Elis** and **Athens** banned Sparta, their enemy, from competing in the Olympics. Despite the ban, a Spartan named **Lichas** entered his chariot, pretending to be from the Egyptian city of **Thebes**. When his chariot won, officials discovered Lichas's trickery and beat him with a rod. That really annoyed the Spartans.

In 416 B.C., with the Spartans still banned from the Olympics, an Athenian general named **Alcibiades** entered seven chariots in the event. One of them won, and two others took second and fourth. Alcibiades threw a huge party, bragging on and on about his success. That annoyed the Spartans even more.

Four Olympics later, Elis and Athens finally let the Spartans compete again. The year was 396 B.C., and Cynisca, close to 50 years old, had waited a long time for this moment. She saw the chariot race as a chance to prove Sparta's superiority. And that's just what she did! Her driver and horses charged up and back on the track for 12 laps and crossed the finish line first.

Cynisca has been hailed as the first female Olympic champion. She marked her achievement by placing a statue of herself at the Olympic site—with these proud words etched in its base:

My ancestors and brothers were kings of Sparta.
I, Cynisca, victorious with a chariot of swift-footed horses,
erected this statue. I declare that I am the only woman
in all of Greece to have won this crown.

A young Cynisca

Women spectators weren't allowed at the Olympics, so it's likely Cynisca never saw her chariot win.

iPuzzle
It's Greek to Me

Fill in a Greek letter and then its name in English so that
each clue is answered. Every Greek letter will be used once.

Α	Ε	Θ	Μ	Ν	Ξ	Π	Ρ	Τ	Φ	Χ	Ψ
~~ALPHA~~	ETA	THETA	MU	NU	XI	PI	RHO	TAU	PHI	CHI	PSI

1. Something used by writers: A   ALPHA BET

2. What you're not: ____   S T U _____ D

3. Difficult way to walk: ____   U _____ L L

4. Hard stuff: ____   M _____ L

5. Acted like a teacher: ____   _____ G H T

6. Dessert with a stick in it: ____   P O _____ C L E

7. Some time: ____   M I _____ T E

8. Computer or ATM: ____   M A _____ N E

9. Not quite LOLing: ____   A _____ S E D

10. It's used to go: ____   E _____ T

EXTRA CREDIT (split each Greek name to form a two-word answer):

11. Beeper on a wheel: ____   C A _____ R N

12. Something that's good to hit: ____   _____ R G E T

What's a Greek's favorite dessert?

Π

Spartan Women: Sparta was known for its mighty
male warriors. But its women were no slouches, either. Spartan
girls had fitness training from age seven. They learned wrestling,
gymnastics, and even combat. Additionally, wealthy girls such
as Cynisca would learn horseback riding and chariot racing.

Jump to this
page **or** follow
the pipes.

Portraits: Polo tile mosaic in Ventimiglia, Italy. Kubla Khan painting by Anige.

1298

I've made my way to a prison cell in **Genoa, Italy**. And look who I've found—the most famous traveler in world history, **Marco Polo**! What's he doing here? It all started with a journey.

Eastward, Ho!

Marco Polo

In 1271, at age 17, Marco Polo set off from **Venice, Italy,** to see the mysterious world of the **Mongols** to the east. He traveled alongside his father and uncle.

The **Mongol Empire** was huge, at one point reaching from **Eastern Europe** all the way across **Asia** to the **Pacific Ocean**. The Polos' journey was a long and difficult one, crossing mountains, desert, and the sea. It took three and a half years for them to reach the leader of the Mongols, **Kublai Khan**. ⟶

Wondrous sights greeted the trio on their trip—large cities with paved roads, a bridge with hundreds of lions carved into it, and Kublai Khan's magnificent palace where a feast for 6,000 people could be held. The Mongol Empire is known as being one the deadliest ever (40 million people killed), but the Mongols also created beautiful artworks: illustrated books, painted tiles, and fine pottery. The Polos were most interested in the silks, jewels, gold, silver, and spices that could make them rich. "Show me the *lire*!" (That's Italian money.)

Twenty-four years passed before the Polos returned to Italy, and, boy, were they in for a surprise! Their hometown of Venice was at war with another Italian city, **Genoa**. Marco joined the battle, and in 1298, the enemy captured him. (Aha!)

While hanging out in a Genoa dungeon, Marco Polo met a fellow prisoner, **Rusticello da Pisi**, who was a writer. The two men began working together. Polo told of his adventures, and da Pisi wrote them down. The result: a book known as *The Travels of Marco Polo*.

One Famous Reader

Christopher Columbus was partly inspired by Marco Polo's book. He sailed west to reach the lands Polo described and discovered the Americas instead.

iPuzzle
Polo Shirts

Which two of Marco's shirts are exactly the same?

What do you call Marco Polo when he's at sea?

Water Polo.

Dog Men: Marco Polo didn't actually visit all the places in *The Travels of Marco Polo*. Some of his tales were based on things he'd heard. Others were added by the book's author, Rusticello da Pisi. One entry described the people of the Andaman Islands in the Indian Ocean. Polo claimed they lived like wild beasts. I guess that's understandable because Polo also said the men had heads like dogs. And, oh yeah, they ate people with human heads!

Jump to this page **or** follow the pipes.

Mongols had far more portraits painted of their horses than themselves.

1904 I just crawled out of a drainpipe near the finish line of the second **Tour de France**, the world's biggest bicycle race. France's **Maurice Garin** has pedaled to victory for the second year in a row... or has he?

Wheely Big Scandal

The very first Tour de France, held in the summer of 1903, was a big success. It consisted of six **stages** (sections of the race held on different days) that took the cyclists in a 1,509-mile (2,428 km) loop around France. Large crowds watched Maurice Garin win, almost three hours ahead of the next finisher— and two and a half *days* in front of the last-place rider!

Maurice Garin

Preparations for the second Tour de France—for both the riders and their fans— apparently included finding every possible way to cheat. When the race ended, the Tour founder, **Henri Desgrange**, said, "The Tour de France is finished, and I'm afraid its second edition has been the last.... We are disgusted, frustrated, and discouraged." What happened?

On the first stage, spectators threw nails in the road. One of the favorites suffered so many flats and crashes that he lost two and a half hours to the leaders. Toward the end of the stage, a carload of masked men tried to run Garin and another top rider off the road. Garin pedaled by and won the stage.

During a climb up a mountain road in the second stage, supporters of one rider attacked Garin and an Italian rider, **Giovanni Gerbi**. Gerbi ended up with several broken fingers and had to drop out of the race. The next day, the riders had to fight off a mob of fans in the town of Nîmes. Tour officials fired a gun in the air to chase them off. Riders had to dodge nails in the road again, as they did in most of the stages.

In the end, Maurice Garin won the race for the second year—but *not*! Race organizers met and, four months later, ruled Garin had received food from an official during the race. Even worse, he and several other riders had taken car and train rides during some of the stages. The top four finishers were disqualified, and the fifth-place rider, a 19-year-old named Henri Cornet, was declared the winner.

iPuzzle
Wheels of Fortune

Starting with the red letter, write down *every other* letter from inside each bicycle tire, traveling in a clockwise direction. (You'll have to go around each tire twice.) The letters will spell out the joke's answer.

Why can't a bicycle stand up on its own?

B _ _ _ _ _ _ _

_ _ _ _ _ _ _ _

_ _ _ _

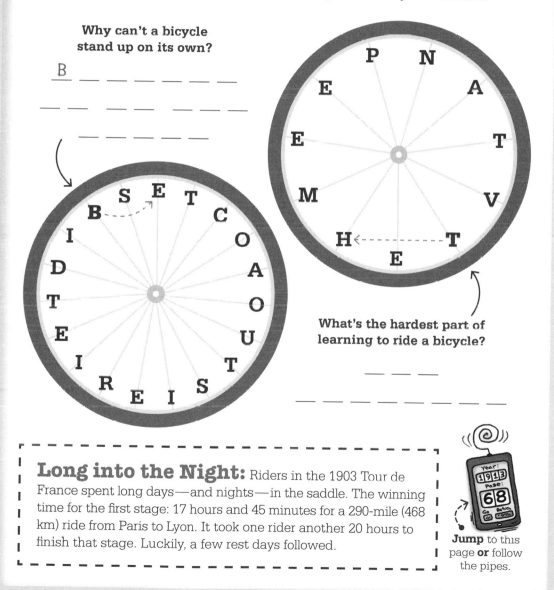

What's the hardest part of learning to ride a bicycle?

_ _ _ _ _ _

Long into the Night: Riders in the 1903 Tour de France spent long days—and nights—in the saddle. The winning time for the first stage: 17 hours and 45 minutes for a 290-mile (468 km) ride from Paris to Lyon. It took one rider another 20 hours to finish that stage. Luckily, a few rest days followed.

Year: 1913 Page: 68

Jump to this page **or** follow the pipes.

1916

I've come aboard *Britannic*, a sister ship of the recently sunk *Titanic.* But I'm not going to stay long because, as you might have heard, rats desert sinking ships. Why do I think that's going to happen? I just spotted **Violet Jessop** on board.

Violet Jessop

Sinking Violet

In 1907, the **White Star Line**, a British shipping company, decided to build a trio of what they called *Olympic*-class ocean liners. These ships would be the largest, fanciest, and safest ships ever built.

Olympic's grand staircase

In 1911, the first ship, ***Olympic***, made its maiden voyage across the **Atlantic Ocean** from England to New York. That trip went well, as did three more. But later that year, a British warship, ***HMS Hawke,*** collided with *Olympic*. It tore two large holes in *Olympic*'s side, flooding parts of the ship. On board *Olympic* as it limped back to port: Violet Jessop, one of the ship's stewardesses.

On April 10, 1912, ***Titanic*** headed out on its maiden voyage. Four days into its journey, the ship hit an **iceberg**. Two hours and forty minutes later, *Titanic* upended and sank in the frigid North Atlantic waters. Of the estimated 2,224 people on board, 1,500 died. Among the staff who made it to safety aboard the lifeboats: Violet Jessop.

By the time *Britannic* was completed in 1914, **World War I** had begun. Britain's **Royal Navy** took control of the ship and converted it to a floating hospital.

Britannic's life was longer than *Titanic*'s, but not by much. On its sixth mission, in 1916, the ship struck a German mine and sank to the bottom of the **Aegean Sea**. Twenty-eight people died, and many others suffered terrible injuries. But guess who ended up treading water? Violet Jessop, now a nurse for the **British Red Cross**. Jessop barely avoided being sucked into the ship's propellers. With a fractured skull and a deep gash in her leg, she clung to two lifejackets until a boat rescued her. Jessop continued working aboard ships for another 27 years and died in 1971 at age 83.

Britannic was built using more than 3 million rivets.

iPuzzle
Pick Trick

Fourteen of the names listed below were actual White Star Line ships. Three weren't. Look for the 14 real names reading forward, backward, up, down, and diagonally. None of the three phonies can be found.

ADRIATIC
ARITHMETIC
ATLANTIC
BALTIC
CELTIC
DORIC
GAELIC
GEORGIC
GERMANIC
HOMERIC
IDIOTIC
MAJESTIC
OCEANIC
PANIC
REPUBLIC
TEUTONIC
TROPIC

```
N B O O S U P O S Z B Y
C F C V O C I R O D A V
J I I H O M E R I C L O
Q N T V L C X L A F T A
B N S A W I U G T C I R
R C E D I G A E L I C E
F I J P J R Z R A L C R
X P A X H O D M N B Q U
S O M L Z E A A T U Y U
V R N C H G X N I P J T
A T E U T O N I C E E X
A O C E A N I C A R E D
```

My Toothbrush! After surviving the *Titanic* disaster, Violet Jessop was very unhappy to find she had no toothbrush to use aboard the rescue ship. So, when *Britannic* started to sink, one of the first things she grabbed from her room was a toothbrush. A day later, while recovering in a seaside hotel that had run out of everything, she took a moment to brush her teeth. When a hotel worker spotted this, she asked in amazement, "Wherever did you get that toothbrush?"

Jump to this page **or** follow the pipes.

1930 Shhh... I just landed in a **soup kitchen** run by gangster **Al "Scarface" Capone** in a poor **Chicago** neighborhood. It's the start of the **Great Depression,** and millions of Americans are out of work. If I want to snatch a bite to eat, I need to be very quiet.

Scarface Soup

Al Capone was one of the worst bad guys ever. He headed a Chicago **crime organization** that made money in all sorts of illegal ways. Also, he killed people (or ordered others to kill them).

Mugshot of Al Capone

On February 14, 1929, Capone masterminded what became known as the **Saint Valentine Day's Massacre**, killing seven rival gang members. That got the attention of the U.S. government. The G-men wanted this crook put in jail, but Capone was sneaky. They couldn't find enough evidence to arrest him, so they started watching him like hawks.

With the law hounding him, Capone decided he needed some good publicity. In 1930, he opened one of Chicago's first **soup kitchens**. Tons of Chicagoans had lost their jobs following the big **stock market collapse** of 1929, and Capone won over many of them by serving meals three times a day. On **Thanksgiving Day** in 1930, the kitchen served beef stew to more than 5,000 people.

Generosity wasn't a new thing for Capone. When he wasn't committing crimes or killing people, he could actually be kind of a nice guy. Capone gave waiters $100 tips. The needy received warm clothes and coal. And, if he heard of a deserving kid who couldn't afford college, he'd pay for it. Because of that, some people saw him as a modern-day **Robin Hood**, taking from the rich and giving to the poor. All the bad stuff he did was invisible to them.

Capone's criminal reign came to an end in 1931, when the U.S. government finally nailed him. What did they get him for? Murder? No. Robbery? No. Capone was found guilty of not paying his taxes and sentenced to 11 years in prison. He died of a heart attack at age 48, a few years after being released.

Photos: Mugshot by U.S. Dept. of Justice. Soup kitchen by U.S. Information Agency.

... Three cuts that Al Capone got in a knife fight as a teenager earned him the nickname Scarface. ...

iPuzzle
Lineup

Two of these photos of Al Capone's soup kitchen are identical. The other two have been altered (each in a different way). Which two match?

The Great Depression: When the stock market crashed in 1929, people lost tons of money, and many companies went out of business. In the United States, nearly 25 percent of workers lost their jobs. One factory after another closed in Chicago. By 1933, Chicago unemployment was nearly 50 percent—twice the national average.

Year: 1936
Page: 54
Go Return

Jump to this page **or** follow the pipes.

... An armored Cadillac that once belonged to Capone was later used by President Franklin Roosevelt.

1608

Wow! Look at the size of this bell. It was worth squeezing through these rusty Burmese pipes to see it. It's called the **Dhammazedi Bell**, and it's the largest ever made. Unfortunately, this is the last anyone will see of it.

Incredi-Bell

The Dhammazedi Bell

Around the year 1480, **King Dhammazedi**, ruler of the **Mon people** of **Burma** (now Myanmar), ordered his ministers to count the kingdom's population. Somehow, they took that to mean the king wanted taxes collected from everyone. The result of their misunderstanding: a 290-ton pile of copper (the people apparently kept a lot of copper around and used it to pay their bills).

When the king found out what had been done, he was not happy. But the work of returning everyone's copper seemed too great, so the ministers hatched an idea. Why not make the world's largest bell with it? The king approved.

On February 5, 1484, the king's bell makers completed their work. They used gold, silver, and tin in addition to the copper and covered the bell's outer surface with writing. Their creation measured more than three adults tall, one standing atop another, and two adults wide, lying down head to toe.

The bell was hung outside the **Shwedagon Pagoda**, a gold-plated **Buddhist shrine**, and stayed there until 1608. By that time, the Portuguese had begun setting up trading posts in the area, and one governor, **Filipe de Brito e Nicote**, had his eye on the bell. He wanted to melt it down to make ship cannons.

De Brito stole the bell by rolling it down a hill, and then hauled it by elephant to the nearby **Bago River**. With the bell atop a raft, he lashed it to his ship and headed downriver. However, as de Brito started across the **Yangon River** to his fortress in **Syriam**, the raft broke up and the bell sank, taking his ship with it.

The bell was never seen again, and soon, neither was de Brito. The Mon people, angry with de Brito's actions, captured and killed him.

iPuzzle
Add a BELL

Each answer below is missing one B, one E, and two L's.
Figure how many of those letters go in each space and in what order.
If you get stuck, try letters in different spots until you get a word.

1. Dining room item: T A _BLE_ C _L_ O T H

2. Candy: J E _____ Y _____ A N

3. People see with it: _____ Y E _____ A _____

4. It's opened and held up: U M _____ R _____ A

5. Where people have "buttons": _____ E _____ I   S

6. Type of dance: _____ A _____ T

7. ____ board (school item): _____ U _____ T I N

8. It's thrown and hit: _____ A S _____ B A _____

9. Can identifier: _____ A _____

EXTRA CREDIT:

10. Part of a word: S Y _____ L A _____

11. Like rubber pencils: F _____ X I _____ E

12. Whale part that sprays: _____ O W H O _____

What do you call someone who falls from the top of a bell tower?

A dead ringer.

Impossi-Bell: Over the years, several diving teams have tried to recover the Dhammazedi Bell from its resting spot at the bottom of the Yangon River. None have succeeded. While the river isn't especially deep, other difficulties exist: 1) bad visibility, 2) other shipwrecks in the area, 3) changing currents, and 4) a thick layer of mud that likely covers the bell.

Year: 1654
Page: 26
Go   Return

Jump to this page **or** follow the pipes.

Campanologist is the technical term for a bell ringer.

Copper has traditionally been used as the main metal to make church bells.

1873 Welcome to **Morristown**, **New Jersey**. Pull up a chair and join me as I look over the shoulder of **Thomas Nast**, the greatest **cartoonist** of his time. Thanks in big part to Nast's work, a crooked New York City politician named **William "Boss" Tweed** has just been tossed in jail.

Nast's Mighty Pen

In Nast's day, **TV** hadn't been invented. Neither had **radio**. People got their news from **newspapers**, but reproducing photos wasn't yet practical. So newspapers used illustrations. In the U.S., more than 10,000 drawings a week appeared in the press. That turned cartoonists and artists into big stars.

"Boss" Tweed by Thomas Nast

Nast drawings from Harper's Weekly.

Nast used his pen to attack dishonest politicians, "Boss" Tweed in particular. Tweed ruled New York City and much of the state, illegally pocketing millions of dollars. Nast pictured him as a thief, a bully, and a clown; and Tweed wanted the drawings stopped. "I don't care what the papers write about me. My constituents [the voters] can't read," Tweed reportedly said, but "they can see pictures!" Nast received threatening letters, and rough-looking men lurked outside his home, but he didn't back down. His drawings continued to expose Tweed's wrongdoing.

Tweed tried another tactic. Nast received an offer to study art in **Europe**, along with $100,000 to cover lost work. Nast pretended interest and asked for $500,000. When Tweed's man agreed, Nast replied, "Well, I don't think I'll do it. I made up my mind not long ago to put some of those fellows behind bars." Public pressure grew, and a few years later, that's exactly what happened. The police arrested Tweed, and he spent his final years in jail, dying there in 1878.

Ho, Ho, Ho!

Nast is probably best known for his Christmas drawings. He was the first artist to draw Santa as we know him today. He also gave Santa a home at the North Pole, invented his workshop and elves, and came up with the idea of writing letters to Santa.

Nast's Santa

Nast was born in Germany and came to the U.S. at age six.

iPuzzle
Party Time

Nast invented the elephant as a symbol for the Republican Party
and popularized the Democratic donkey. Using only the letters
in REPUBLICAN or DEMOCRATIC, fill in the blanks below.

REPUBLICAN

Republican elephant
worn out from
fighting
Democrats

1. Find three 3-letter words starting with L:

_____   _____   _____

2. Four 4-letter words starting with B:

_____   _____   _____   _____

3. One 5-letter word starting with P: _____

EXTRA CREDIT: Any 6-letter word: _____

Nast's first use of
the Democratic
donkey →

DEMOCRATIC

1. Find three 3-letter words starting with R:

_____   _____   _____

2. Four 4-letter words starting with C:

_____   _____   _____   _____

3. One 5-letter word starting with T: _____

EXTRA CREDIT: Any 6-letter word: _____

Gotcha! Shortly after "Boss" Tweed was thrown in jail, he
escaped and made his way to Spain. He might have stayed there,
but Spanish officials recognized him from one of Nast's drawings
and arrested him. And do you know what the U.S. authorities
found in Tweed's luggage after the Spanish turned him over?
A complete collection of every cartoon Nast had drawn of him!

Jump to this
page **or** follow
the pipes.

Nast couldn't read or write. His wife, or people he hired, read to him as he drew.

1788 I've piped myself aboard a ship in the **First Fleet**. That's a group of 11 English ships taking colonists, prisoners, supplies, and animals to **Australia**. Among the animals are five **European rabbits**. Not many, is it? But just wait. Here comes the…

Invasion of the Bunnies

Captain James Cook, an English explorer, visited Australia while sailing the Pacific in 1770. He named the southeast corner of it **New South Wales**. That's where the First Fleet landed 18 years later to start a colony, open a prison, and raise some rabbits (as well as sheep, chickens, horses, and other critters).

The rabbits did well in the new land, and their numbers increased slowly until 1859. That's when a man named **Thomas Austin** decided to release 24 rabbits into the wild. "The introduction of a few rabbits could do little harm and might provide a touch of home, in addition to a spot of hunting," Austin reasoned.

Wrong! Within 40 years, the eastern half of Australia was home to a billion bunnies! Yes, billion. Native animals, such as **wombats** and **bandicoots**, suffered as the rabbits ate up their food and moved into their burrows. **Mulga** trees and plants such as the **emu bush** began disappearing thanks to the rabbits' constant munching. These cute little bunnies were a natural disaster.

In 1901, the government, hoping to stop the hungry hoppers' westward expansion, built a **Rabbit-Proof Fence**. Workers erected a waist-high barrier that stretched all the way across the country, more than 1,100-miles (1,800 km). But it didn't work. Neither did a second fence—or a third. The bunnies kept coming, and by 1920, they numbered 10 billion.

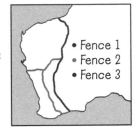

- Fence 1
- Fence 2
- Fence 3

Ranchers trapped and shot the rabbits, but they couldn't keep pace with females that produced up to 30 young per year. Finally, in 1950, officials introduced a rabbit disease from South America, which greatly reduced the bunny population. Another disease, brought in from China in 1995, also worked. But 200 million rabbits live on, and their numbers have started to rebound in recent years.

iPuzzle
Fence Defense

If you wanted to stop this rabbit from getting to the carrot, in which of these spots (more than one) would you need to add fence sections?

Why? European rabbits have lived in Europe for thousands of years and didn't harm it the way they did Australia. One big reason: predators. Europe had lynxes, eagles, and other animals that loved rabbit for lunch. Australia didn't, really. Also, Europe had rabbit diseases, rabbit hunters, and in modern times, fewer and fewer places for the rabbits to live.

Jump to this page **or** follow the pipes.

1739 I love a good library. That's why I've come to the **Royal Library** in **Dresden, Germany,** to see the latest addition, a Mayan book known as the **Dresden Codex**. This book's just my style— all pictures!

Oh My, Maya!

I'm going to start right off by showing you two of the 78 pages from this book because … well, they're amazing. Sure, they've gotten dirty and scuffed up over the years, but it's a miracle they still exist at all.

The **Maya people** of **Central America** created this book sometime after A.D. 1210 (that's the most recent date in it). They used **fig tree** bark to make the paper, drew the pictures with ink made from soot, and colored it using natural materials, such as rust for the red. One really cool thing: although it's 12 feet long (3.5 m) when fully opened, it can fold up accordion-style to fit in your hand.

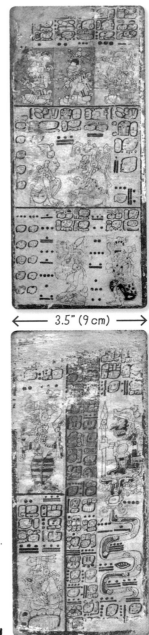

← 3.5" (9 cm) →

The book contains astronomy, calendars, weather, religion, and pictures of Mayan gods. According to Mayan and Spanish records, thousands of similar books were created, but this is one of only three (maybe four) that still exist. What happened to all the others?

In the 16th century, when **Spanish explorers** saw the Mayan books, they considered them to be the work of the devil. Priests burned piles of them in bonfires. Others were tossed in the ocean as valueless. :-(

The Dresden Codex survived and made it to Europe. Some suggest **Hernán Cortés,** the Spanish explorer, brought it as a gift to the king of Spain, but nobody's sure. There's a second Mayan codex in Paris and a third in Madrid. A fourth, called the **Grolier Codex**, was found in a Mexican cave in 1965, although some people think it's a fake.

Having crossed eyes was a desirable trait among the Mayans.

iPuzzle
Maya Match

To decode each Mayan symbol, solve the Mayan math problem next to it.
The solution will match the number of the correct meaning in the bottom box.

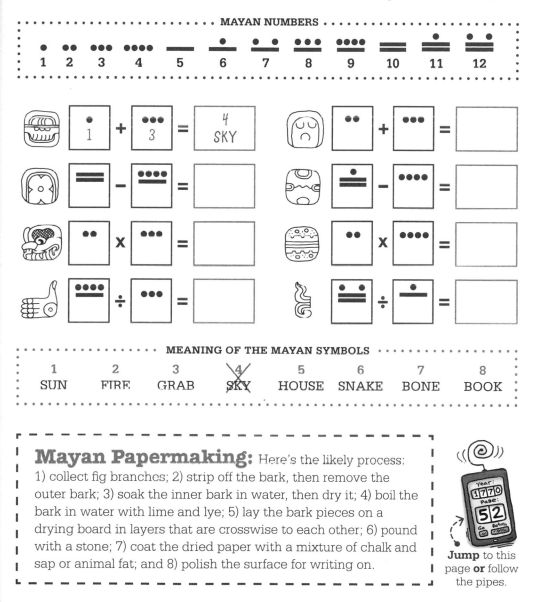

MAYAN NUMBERS

| 1 | 2 | 3 | 4 | 5 | 6 | 7 | 8 | 9 | 10 | 11 | 12 |

MEANING OF THE MAYAN SYMBOLS

1	2	3	4	5	6	7	8
SUN	FIRE	GRAB	SKY	HOUSE	SNAKE	BONE	BOOK

Mayan Papermaking: Here's the likely process:
1) collect fig branches; 2) strip off the bark, then remove the outer bark; 3) soak the inner bark in water, then dry it; 4) boil the bark in water with lime and lye; 5) lay the bark pieces on a drying board in layers that are crosswise to each other; 6) pound with a stone; 7) coat the dried paper with a mixture of chalk and sap or animal fat; and 8) polish the surface for writing on.

Year: 1770
Page: 52
Go   Return

Jump to this page **or** follow the pipes.

1654 Forget horror movies. I've made my way to one of the creepiest places anywhere—**Hart Island**. A doctor named **Thomas Pell** has just bought it from the **Siwanoy Indians**, and it's a beautiful spot of land in the **Long Island Sound**. That will soon change.

Creepsville

1/4 mile
(400 m)

Pell's purchase, reportedly paid for with casks of rum, was part of a package that included most or all of the Bronx and other land along the coast. His heirs sold the island in 1774, which then changed hands several more times over the next 50 years. And then the weirdness began....

• In the early 1800s, **bare-knuckle boxing** matches took place on Hart Island. As many of 6,000 "loafers and rowdies" (as one reporter described them) sailed to the island for the bloody fights.

• In the 1860s, during the **Civil War**, the federal government built a prison camp on Hart Island The army crammed more than 3,000 Confederate prisoners into it, two men to a bunk. Hundreds died from disease, lack of food, and the cold.

• In 1868, New York City paid $75,000 so it could use part of the island to bury poor and unidentified people. The graveyard's population now stands at 850,000, making it the largest government-owned cemetery in the world. Inmates from nearby **Rikers Island** took over the gravedigging duties in the 1930s. Those prisoners, nicknamed the "Ghoul Squad," actually looked forward to the job. They sometimes needed to wear masks because dead bodies reek, but the work got them out of jail for the day.

• But wait—there's more! The island has also been home to an isolation ward for **yellow fever** victims, a facility for drug addicts, a **missile base**, a hospital for insane women, a homeless shelter, and a workhouse for "vicious boys." These vicious boys, actually just homeless orphans, learned trades at a school built on the island. And according to *The New York Times*, if they behaved themselves during the week, "the teachers let them have a half-holiday on Saturday afternoons to go out and play among the graves."

The islands on these two pages are all in scale to one another.

iPuzzle
Island-Hopping

Which one of these New York City islands did Dwayne NOT visit after his trip to Hart Island? Check off the islands he *did* visit, until there's only one left.

Dwayne visited an island...

...with no R's in its name.

...with three R's in its name.

...that spells a word backward.

...with punctuation in its name.

...whose name includes the 25th letter of the alphabet.

...with "IN" in its name.

...with more A–F letters in its name than G–Z letters.

...whose letters can be rearranged to spell TOOTHBRUSHER.

☐ PRALL'S
☐ LIBERTY

Statue of Liberty

☐ NORTH BROTHER

☐ SWINBURNE

☐ SOUTH BROTHER

☐ RUFFLE BAR   ☐ RAT

☐ ELLIS

☐ MILL ROCK

Hartland! In 1925, Solomon Riley owned a four-acre chunk of Hart Island and started building an amusement park on it. He got as far as putting up a dance hall, some boarding houses, and 200 feet of boardwalk before New York City bought him out and stopped the project. Why? The city operated a prison next door to it and worried that prisoners would escape.

Year: 1739
Page: 24

Jump to this page **or** follow the pipes.

... U Thant Island, in New York City's East River, is only about two-thirds the size of a football field. ...

1888

I've inched up to peek into an ancient pit a farmer just uncovered near **Istabl Antar, Egypt**. Yikes! It's filled with hundreds of thousands of...

Mummy Cats

Well, at least they're dead. And they've been that way for more than 2,000 years. But how'd they all get here?

The **ancient Egyptians** loved making mummies. A mummy maker would remove most of the innards from a dead body, preserve the dried body with salt, then wrap it in linen.

Sometimes, mummified people would be buried with their mummified pets. There might even be mummified food for them to snack on. (Yum!) Why all this mummifying? The Egyptians thought it would allow the **ka**, the soul of the dead person or animal, to recognize its dead body and start a second life in it.

Cats were sacred to the Egyptians. They represented **Bastet**, a goddess of good fortune. When a pet cat died, its owners would mourn for it, and maybe even mummify it. But this huge pit of mummy cats wasn't just a bunch of pets.

The Egyptians also sacrificed cats to honor Bastet. They raised huge numbers of cats for just that purpose. The cats would then be elaborately mummified. Linen strips would be dyed in two colors and woven in patterns. Painted masks might be placed over the cats' faces. Some cat mummies would be placed in cat-shaped **coffins** decorated with gold. That explains the hundreds of thousands of mummy cats in this pit—they were sacrificial cats.

After the discovery of the mummy cats, word quickly spread. Local kids dug through the pile to find the best mummies and sold them to **tourists**. Some eventually ended up in museums. But, weirdest of all, many of the

mummies were sold as **fertilizer** (they were rich in nutrients, such as nitrogen, that plants need). One ship loaded up 180,000 mummy cats (19 tons worth), and hauled them to London to be used for growing crops. The price: about $350.

iPuzzle
Cats!

Each answer below contains the word CAT. We've drawn a cat's head in its place—you need to fill in the rest. To help, the missing letters for each answer are listed at the bottom (in order, minus CAT).

1. Comic strip that's named for a woman: 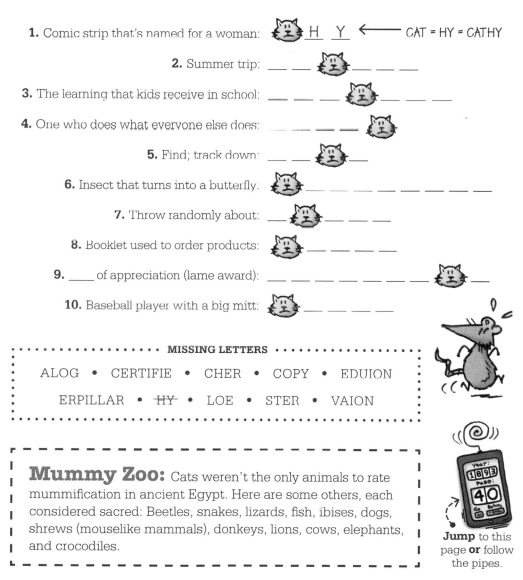 H Y ⟵ CAT = HY = CATHY

2. Summer trip: __ __ __ __ __

3. The learning that kids receive in school: __ __ __ __ __ __

4. One who does what everyone else does: __ __ __ __ __

5. Find; track down: __ __ __ __

6. Insect that turns into a butterfly: __ __ __ __ __ __ __ __

7. Throw randomly about: __ __ __ __ __

8. Booklet used to order products: __ __ __ __

9. ____ of appreciation (lame award): __ __ __ __ __ __ __ __ __

10. Baseball player with a big mitt: __ __ __ __ __

· · · · · · · · · · · · · · **MISSING LETTERS** · · · · · · · · · · · · · ·

ALOG • CERTIFIE • CHER • COPY • EDUION

ERPILLAR • ~~HY~~ • LOE • STER • VAION

Mummy Zoo: Cats weren't the only animals to rate mummification in ancient Egypt. Here are some others, each considered sacred: Beetles, snakes, lizards, fish, ibises, dogs, shrews (mouselike mammals), donkeys, lions, cows, elephants, and crocodiles.

Jump to this page **or** follow the pipes.

In 525 B.C., the Persians conquered Egypt by marching with cats in their arms, which the Egyptians wouldn't risk killing.

1969

The iSwirl couldn't get me aboard *Apollo 11*, which is sending the first two men to the **Moon**. But it could get me into NASA's **Mission Control** in **Houston, Texas**. Shhh…let's see if we can hear what the astronauts are saying.

Moonspeak

Aldrin's moon bootprint ➡

Photos courtesy of NASA.

What were the first words broadcast from the Moon? That's not so easy to answer. On July 20, when the *Eagle* lunar module landed on the Moon, Commander **Neil Armstrong** radioed back these famous words, "Houston…Tranquility Base here. The *Eagle* has landed."

But Armstrong's announcement came about 14 seconds after the *Eagle* set down. In the meantime, Armstrong's crewmate **Buzz Aldrin** had already been chatting it up with Earth. He started with, "Okay. Engine stop," and then spewed out five more sentences of technical mumbo jumbo. Only then did Armstrong pipe in with his much-quoted remark. Because of that, some people think Aldrin's "okay" was the first word from the Moon.

↰ Aldrin on the Moon

All right, so that's a bit murky. But surely, there's no doubt about the first words spoken when Neil Armstrong went for a walk on the Moon. Wrong!

About seven hours after *Eagle* landed, Armstrong opened the hatch, made his way down the ladder, and hopped onto the Moon's powdery surface. He then stated to a worldwide TV audience of 500 million people, "That's one small step for man, one giant leap for mankind."

Except that's not what he meant to say…and not what he claimed he said. According to Armstong, he said, "That's one small step for *a* man, one giant leap for mankind." It makes a difference, because "man" without "a" in front of it means the same thing as "mankind." Some officials backed up Armstrong, claiming static covered up the missing "a." But, listening to the tape, it sounds more like he just goofed.

There are almost no pictures of Neil Armstrong on the Moon because he had the only camera.

iPuzzle
Apollo 1-11

Number these 11 NASA photos in the order they happened, from first to last. A timeline of events is listed below to help you if needed.

Apollo 11 Timeline:
April 18: Neil Armstrong does some simulation training. **July 16:** launch day. **July 20:** the *Eagle* separates from the *Columbia* and lands on the Moon. **July 21:** Armstrong walks on the Moon, then photographs Buzz Aldrin coming down to join him. *Eagle*'s top half lifts off (photographed by a camera left on the Moon) and links back up with *Columbia*. **July 24:** *Columbia*'s capsule lands in the Pacific Ocean and is lifted aboard the USS *Hornet*, where the astronauts are isolated in case they have Moon germs. **August 13:** New York City gives the astronauts a ticker-tape parade.

Jump to this page **or** follow the pipes.

1807 Quick, who's the most successful pirate ever? Blackbeard? Red Beard? Captain Jack Sparrow? No, it's **Ching Shih**, and I'm aboard one of *her* junks (Chinese ships) in the **South China Sea**.

Ching Shih's flag

The Widow Pirate

郑氏 郑氏

Ching Shih didn't start out as a pirate. Until 1801, she was a landlubber (non-sea person) in **Guangzhou, China**. But when a dashing pirate captain named **Zheng Yi** swept into town and proposed marriage, she said yes—under one condition: She wanted to be an equal partner in his pirating business. Zheng Yi agreed, heading back to sea with a new bride and co-captain at his side.

The **Red Flag Fleet** grew under the pair's leadership. No ship or town in southeast China was safe. In 1807, however, a huge storm took Zheng Yi's life, sending him to **Davy Jones's Locker** (the bottom of the sea). But that didn't stop Ching. She named her first mate as captain but masterminded the whole operation herself. The Red Flag Fleet soon numbered more than 1,500 junks and 60,000 pirates—one of the largest navies in the world.

Keeping that many outlaws in line is a tricky job. So Ching created tough new punishments. Sneaking ashore twice without permission: beheading. Stealing from the ship's haul of treasure: beheading. Violence against a woman or wedding her without permission: beheading.

Those pirates with heads still on their necks kept the Red Flag Fleet in control of the coast in all directions. They attacked—Chinese, Portuguese, and British ships alike. They also demanded payments from villages in exchange for protection (from not being killed by the pirates).

The Chinese government tried everything to stop Ching's pirate fleet. Nothing worked. Finally, in 1810, officials came up with a solution. If Ching would retire, she could go free and keep all her loot. The same would be true for most of her pirates. *Cha-Ching*! She agreed, invested her fortune in a gambling house and smuggling ring, and lived happily ever after until 1844.

The typical Chinese pirate junk had three sails and rows of oars on both sides.

Chinese pirate swords could cut through metal armor.

iPuzzle
Pirate Search

Avast, ye swabs (止住, 海盗)! Look for the names of these 17 real and fictional pirates reading forward, backward, up, down, and diagonally.

AVERY
BARBAROSSA
BLACKBEARD
BLOOD
BONNY
CHIVERS
DRAKE
HOOK
KIDD
LAFITTE
MORGAN
O'MALLEY
RACKHAM
READ
ROBERTS
SILVER
SPARROW

```
W K A H Y H Z D M T A V
Y N N O B L O O D F U M
Y Q R O L M A A C I S U
S D K K A Y E F H M K Y
Y I Y L C R K O I G V R
S M L N K E A H V T K O
V E M V B V R G E I T B
Y M O C E A D K R S E E
B A R B A R O S S A L R
R V G O R A C K H A M T
E X A Z D W O R R A P S
M I N Z G A Z Y T T N S
```

iPuzzle Quickie

Match up the jokes and punch lines.

1. ___ What do Chinese pirates eat?

3. ___ What are the only notes a pirate can sing?

2. ___ What do you call pirates who paint?

A. High C's.

B. Arrrrtists.

C. Junk food.

Jump to this page **or** follow the pipes.

Year: 1812
Page: 76

Many pirates wore pierced earrings thinking it would improve their eyesight.

1899 Welcome to **Syracuse, New York**. We're at the **Merrell-Soule** company, where **Klim** powdered milk has just been invented. Little does the company know, but 45 years from now, 76 prisoners will escape from a **POW (prisoner-of-war) camp** in Germany with the help of 1,400…

Klim Cans

Klim ("milk" spelled backward) is powdered **whole milk**. Big sprayers shoot milk into a stream of hot air. The heat evaporates the water, leaving a fine powder. Tin cans of the milk powder can then be shipped anywhere.

During World War II, the **U.S. Army** thought Klim was the perfect thing for its soldiers. The army's **jungle ration** (on-the-go food pack) included Klim alongside salted beef, dried biscuits, fruit bars, and…toilet paper.

The **Red Cross** also regularly included cans of Klim in packages for British and American POWs. For the prisoners of **Stalag Luft III**, a POW camp near **Berlin**, those cans were especially welcome. The prisoners used them in their escape tunnels—as scoops, candleholders, and ventilation pipes.

Three tunnels—nicknamed Tom, Dick, and Harry—were secretly under construction at Stalag Luft III. They measured two feet wide (0.6 m), two feet high, and up to a football field in length. Breathing posed a big problem. The solution: remove the tops and bottoms of Klim cans, then fit them together to form ventilation pipes running along each tunnel. Hand-operated **pumps** made of boxes and backpacks kept the air moving.

Guards discovered Tom, and a camp extension was built over Dick, but in March 1944, Harry was completed. After waiting for a really dark night, 76 prisoners (mostly British officers) made it through the tunnel on a wheeled trolley cart, out a hole beyond the camp's fence, and off into the woods. Unfortunately, the 77th escapee was spotted outside the fence and immediately captured. Everyone else ran for it.

A nationwide alert went out, and only three made it to safety. The **German secret police** killed 50 and sent the other 23 back to prison camps. Despite that, once things died down, the prisoners at Stalag Luft III began work on a new tunnel. They named it George.

Whole milk is 87 percent water.

iPuzzle
Klim Cards

Look carefully to find eight differences between these two store displays.

Try saying this three times fast: TIN KLIM CANS

Klim-actic: After coming up with the process for creating Klim, the Merrell-Soule company had one problem. Spraying the milk created static electricity, and the powder had a habit of exploding. The solution: dangle strips of tin foil in front of the sprayer, eliminating the static charge.

Year: 1902
Page: 74

Jump to this page **or** follow the pipes.

A movie about the Luft Stalag III escape, titled *The Great Escape*, was made in 1963.

With 200 inches of rain a year (500 cm), New Guinea's jungles are among the wettest places on Earth.

1974

I've piped myself to the island of **New Guinea** in the Pacific Ocean because I'd heard that some of the tribes here live in **treehouses**. And, holy hickory, look at that—it's true!

Tree Tribe

This is one of the coolest things I've ever seen. The **Korowai** are the only people in the world who live in treehouses, and some of their homes are as high up as a 10-story building.

Why treehouses? It helps the Korowai avoid three things: flooding (they get a ton of rain), biting insects, and—get this— enemy clans that might eat them! The Korowai are one of the world's few remaining **cannibal** tribes. They claim they don't eat *people*. They only eat *khakhua* from rival clans, male witches who are no longer human.

It wasn't until 1974 that outsiders first visited the Korowai and wrote about them. A scientific expedition of five men exchanged gifts and knowledge with 35 Korowai hunters (they pointed to things to learn each other's language). Luckily, the Korowai saw the outsiders as merely *laleo* ("demon-ghosts") and not khakhua, so the visitors didn't end up as meals. :-)

Later expeditions followed, discovering how the Korowai built their lofty homes. The tribe members would chose a tree (or several trees close together) and attach a ladder to it. They'd build a platform in the higher branches, sometimes with poles extending down to the ground for extra support. Tree-bark flooring and a palm-leaf roof finished things off. In bigger treehouses, the men and women got separate rooms, with pet dogs and pigs hanging out wherever they could find a spot. Meals were cooked inside, with the remains of the fire glowing through the night to keep everyone warm.

iPuzzle
Treehouse Maze

Get from the jungle floor to the treehouse.

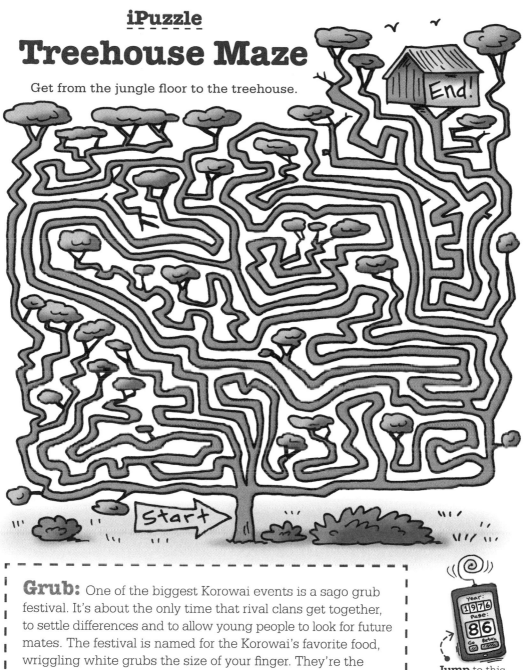

Grub: One of the biggest Korowai events is a sago grub festival. It's about the only time that rival clans get together, to settle differences and to allow young people to look for future mates. The festival is named for the Korowai's favorite food, wriggling white grubs the size of your finger. They're the larvae of capricorn beetles and are eaten both raw and cooked.

Year: 1976
Page: 86
Go   Return

Jump to this page **or** follow the pipes.

1156
I've taken a front-row seat on a bank of the **Isar River** in **Germany** to watch a bishop and duke fighting over…

The Salt Road

The salt road across the Isar River

People can't live without salt. Knowing that, many clever rulers over the years have found ways to make piles of money from it. That's why salt became known as "white gold."

In the 12th century, a German bishop named **Otto von Freising** earned most of his money from salt. He controlled a bridge on the Isar River, and traders carting loads of salt from the mines near **Salzburg, Austria,** to **Augsburg, Germany,** paid him a tax to cross the bridge. People called this route the *Salzstrasse*, or "salt road."

A powerful duke named **Henry the Lion** also lived in the area. Henry had been looking to create a new city on the Isar, but how to pay for it? He couldn't help but notice the easy money that Bishop von Freising made with his salt tax. So he came up with a plan that was startlingly simple.

Henry burned down the bishop's bridge and built his own bridge a few miles up the river. He then started collecting the tax himself.

Harrumph! Bishop von Freising was none too happy about that. So he went right to the top—squawking to his nephew, **Emperor Frederick Barbarossa**. You might think the emperor would side with his uncle, but he didn't. Instead, he approved what his cousin, Henry the Lion, had done. (Wait—did you get that? These guys were all related. Hee-hee.) The emperor set one condition: Henry would have to pay Bishop von Freising a third of all the money he collected.

Henry the Lion did as he was told, and in 1158, the duke used his salt-tax money to build a new city on the land surrounding the bridge. He called it **Munich**— now the third largest city in Germany.

Salzburg means "salt city."

An adult's body contains enough salt to fill a coffee mug.

iPuzzle
A Dash of Salt

NaCl is the chemical symbol for salt.
Use one N, one A, one C, and one L to complete *each pair* of words.

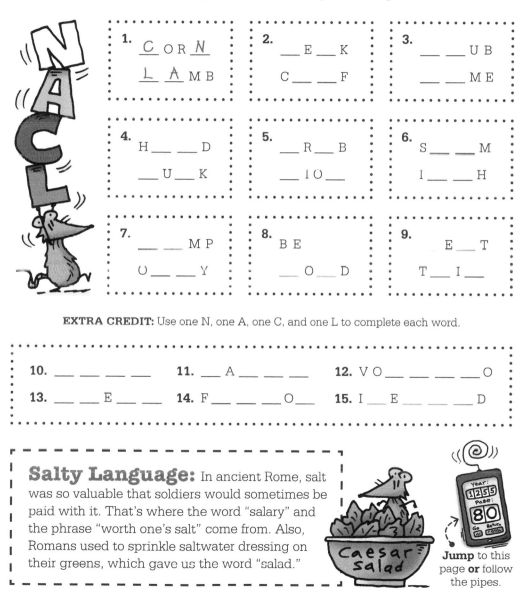

1.
C O R _N_
_L_ _A_ M B

2.
_ _ E _ _ K
C _ _ _ _ F

3.
_ _ _ _ U B
_ _ _ _ M E

4.
H _ _ _ _ D
_ _ U _ _ K

5.
_ _ R _ _ B
_ _ I O _ _

6.
S _ _ _ _ M
I _ _ _ _ H

7.
_ _ _ _ M P
U _ _ _ _ Y

8.
B E
_ _ O _ _ D

9.
_ E _ _ T
T _ _ I _ _

EXTRA CREDIT: Use one N, one A, one C, and one L to complete each word.

10. _ _ _ _ _ _ _ _

11. _ _ A _ _ _ _ _ _

12. V O _ _ _ _ _ _ _ _ O

13. _ _ _ _ E _ _ _ _

14. F _ _ _ _ _ O _ _

15. I _ _ E _ _ _ _ _ _ D

Salty Language:
In ancient Rome, salt was so valuable that soldiers would sometimes be paid with it. That's where the word "salary" and the phrase "worth one's salt" come from. Also, Romans used to sprinkle saltwater dressing on their greens, which gave us the word "salad."

Caesar salad

Jump to this page **or** follow the pipes.

1893 I'm sailing again, this time aboard the *Oneida* with **President Grover Cleveland** and a team of doctors.

Operation Rubber Jaw

In early 1893, voters had just elected Grover Cleveland president. The country was in terrible shape—the government didn't have much money, banks and companies were dropping like flies, and people wandered the streets in search of work.

Oneida

That would be a bad time for the president to say, "Hey, everybody, I've got cancer," wouldn't it? Unfortunately, that was the case—doctors had just discovered a growth in President Cleveland's mouth. An operation to remove it had to be done right away, so a secret plan was hatched.

On July 1, at a dock in **New York City**, the president, five doctors, and a dentist sneaked aboard the *Oneida*. The pilot cranked up its steam engine, and the ship headed up the **East River**. Passing a big hospital along the shore, the doctors all ducked into the cabin, fearing someone might recognize them.

A little after noon, with the president stretched out on an operating table in the ship's main cabin, the medical team went to work. The dentist started by pulling out two teeth. The doctors then took over, removing Cleveland's entire left upper jaw and part of the roof of his mouth. It took about an hour.

The *Oneida* then headed out to sea and up to **Gray Gables**, the president's summer home in **Cape Cod, Massachusetts**. There, another doctor fitted Cleveland with a fancy new jaw made of **vulcanized rubber**—the same stuff that's used to make bowling balls, car tires, and hockey pucks.

A month later, after a quick follow-up operation (again aboard *Oneida*), Cleveland gave a speech to **Congress**, and nobody was the wiser. Oh sure, reporters suspected something, but 24 years would pass before the truth came out.

← Grover Cleveland from an 1892 issue of *Judge* magazine

The *Oneida* was later converted into a tugboat.

iPuzzle
Grover: Yes or No?

Which of these statements about Grover Cleveland are true? Take a guess by writing YES or NO in each blank. Then follow the line to see if you're right.

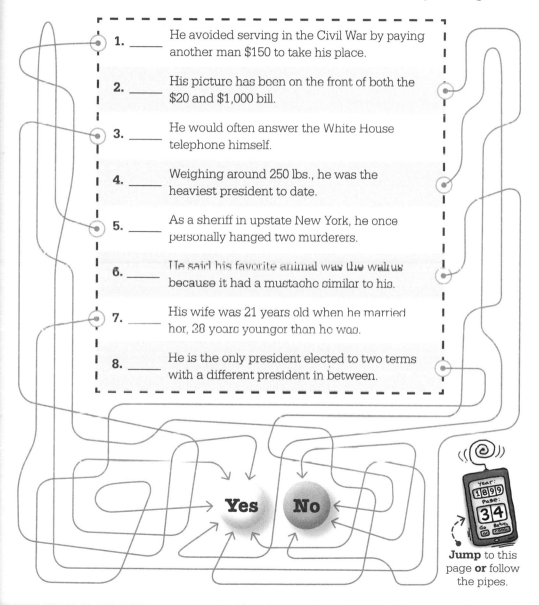

1. _____ He avoided serving in the Civil War by paying another man $150 to take his place.

2. _____ His picture has been on the front of both the $20 and $1,000 bill.

3. _____ He would often answer the White House telephone himself.

4. _____ Weighing around 250 lbs., he was the heaviest president to date.

5. _____ As a sheriff in upstate New York, he once personally hanged two murderers.

6. _____ He said his favorite animal was the walrus because it had a mustache similar to his.

7. _____ His wife was 21 years old when he married her, 28 years younger than he was.

8. _____ He is the only president elected to two terms with a different president in between.

Yes   No

Year: 1899
Page: 34
Go Return

Jump to this page **or** follow the pipes.

CLEVER GOVERN LAD is an anagram of GROVER CLEVELAND.

1000 *Brrr*, it's cold in the North Atlantic. I've just landed on the shores of **North America** with a boatload of **Vikings** led by…

Leif the Lucky

Leif's likely route

In 960, a Viking named **Thorvald** was kicked out of **Norway**. He'd gotten mixed up in a fight, which resulted in a couple of dead Vikings. Thorvald packed up his family, sailed west, and found a nice spot in **Iceland** to call home.

In 982, Thorvald's son, **Erik the Red**, got himself kicked out of Iceland for the exact same reason—a couple of dead Vikings. Erik packed up his family, sailed west, and set up home in **Greenland**.

In 1000, Erik the Red son's, **Leif Eriksson**, sailed west from Greenland—but not because of any dead Vikings. Leif had heard good land lay to the west and, like any respectable Viking, he went off to explore.

The first land that Leif and his men spotted was covered in ice, with large rock slabs along the shore. He named it Slab Land (that's what the Viking word **Helluland** translates to). After a quick stop on Slab Land, making him the first known European to set foot in North America, Leif and his men headed south.

Their next stop was Forest Land, or **Markland**. It had white sandy beaches and lots of trees. Forest Land looked pretty good, but Leif kept sailing. Two days later, he found an even nicer place. He named it **Vinland** after the grapevines he found there. Leif and the others built a few houses and stayed the winter.

In the spring, Leif returned to Greenland. After he told his brothers, **Thorvald** and **Thorstein**, about Vinland, they wanted to see it for themselves. Alas, two separate trips to Vinland turned them into a couple of dead Vikings.

In 1006, a third Viking, **Thorfinn**, sailed to Vinland to start a colony, but his group didn't do so well, either. They got into battles with the local Indians, and were so badly outnumbered, they left and never came back. No other Vikings followed.

Leif Eriksson got his "lucky" nickname after rescuing 15 sailors and being rewarded with their ship's cargo. …

The *Norse* word *Viking* means explorer or pirate.

iPuzzle
Current Events

Following the ocean currents, can you find the one way from Greenland to Vinland?

A Vinland Village: In 1960, two Norwegian archaeologists, Helge and Anne Ingestad, unearthed a small village of Viking buildings on the Canadian island of Newfoundland. The spot, known as *L'Anse aux Meadows*, matches descriptions of Vinland from Viking sagas (tales).

Jump to this page **or** follow the pipes.

1775 America's **Founding Fathers** have gathered in **Philadelphia** for the **Second Continental Congress.** And they've invited a group of **Iroquois** chiefs to stop by. I've hopped up on a chair to get a better view.

"Brave" New World

Surprised to see Iroquois leaders hanging out here? The truth is, a number of America's Founding Fathers respected the **Iroquois Confederacy**, a 400-year-old union of five, then six, Indian nations.

The Iroquois Confederacy offered a great example of the sort of government that could work for the colonies. Each nation handled its own matters, but their chiefs met in a **grand council** to settle larger issues, such as peace treaties and trade agreements. However, the grand council's decisions still needed the approval of two separate councils, and a speaker for them, within each nation. The power was divided, and everyone had a say.

Thirty-one years earlier, **Canassatego**, an Iroquois chief, had offered this advice to the colonists: "We are a powerful Confederacy and by your observing the same methods our wise forefathers have taken, you will acquire much strength and power." In 1775, the Second Continental Congress commissioners remembered that, telling the invited chiefs, "Our forefathers rejoiced to hear Canassatego speak these words. They sunk deep into our hearts."

In 1787, when the **U.S. Constitution** was being put together, **Thomas Jefferson** wrote, "I am convinced that those societies (as the Indians) which live without government enjoy in their general mass an infinitely greater degree of happiness than those who live under European governments."

John Adams especially liked how the Iroquois divided power, and his model of a government with three branches was used in the Constitution.

In 1988, the **U.S. Congress** passed a resolution that formally acknowledged "the contribution of the Iroquois Confederacy of Nations to the development of the U.S. Constitution."

The approved Great Seal sketch

The Iroquois were big farmers. Their main crops were beans, corn, and squash.

iPuzzle
Clan Scan

For each phrase below, there's an anagram in the box (the same letters in a different order). Write the anagram in the blank, then circle which of the two you think is an actual name of an Indian clan listed in the Great Law of Peace.

· · · · · · · · · · · · · · · · · · **ANAGRAMS** · · · · · · · · · · · · · · · · · ·

TWO TOP LADIES • NEATER CABIN • PAINTED TURTLE

LEG ROVER PAL • STANDING ROCK • PIGEON HAWK

PONIES, DEEP FISH, HOT TOAD • GREAT NAME BEARER

_____ **1.** OPPOSITE SIDE OF THE HAND

_____ **2.** RARE BEET MANAGER

_____ **3.** HEAPING WOK

_____ **4.** WILD POTATOES

_____ **5.** ANCIENT BEAR

_____ **6.** PUTTIED ANTLER

_____ **7.** LARGE PLOVER

_____ **8.** DANCING STORK

> Hmm, that last one is kind of a tough choice.

• The Great Seal: The Iroquois Confederacy symbol was an eagle atop the tree of great peace, and a bundle of arrows represented the unity of the six nations. On June 20, 1782, a design for the Great Seal of the United States was approved by Congress. It featured an eagle with an olive branch, a symbol of peace, in one foot and a bundle of arrows in the other.

Jump to this page **or** follow the pipes.

The final version of the Great Seal can be seen on the back of a $1 bill.

1842

I'm in **Mexico City**, just in time for a big celebration. President Santa Anna's leg is being paraded through the streets.

Funeral for a Leg

In 1838, a small war erupted between **France** and **Mexico**. When French soldiers captured the port town of **Veracruz**, General Santa Anna and his men came charging in to save the day. Alas, he was easily defeated, and even worse, the lower half of his left leg had to be amputated (cut off) after being hit by French cannon fire. Still, the Mexican people hailed him as a hero for his courage. His leg received a burial with full military honors at his home, **Manga de Clavo**.

1847 portrait of Santa Anna by A. Hoffy

In 1841, Santa Anna was elected **president** of Mexico. A year later, he decided his leg deserved a more formal ceremony. So he had the limb dug up, paraded through Mexico City, and buried in a fancy monument in the **cemetery of Santa Paula**. Poems, speeches, and cannon fire accompanied the grand occasion.

Santa Anna's popularity didn't last long. In 1844, annoyed with his strict rule and tax increases, angry Mexicans threw him out of office. They then tore down the monument and stole the leg, which was never seen again.

Santa Anna's leg woes weren't over, however. After having his leg amputated in 1838, he'd been outfitted with a fake limb made of wood and cork. It, too, would end up in enemy hands.

In 1847, Santa Anna was back to being a general, and Mexico was at war again, this time with the U.S. One day, in Cerro Gordo, Mexico, Santa Anna took a break to enjoy a chicken lunch. He'd removed his fake leg to be more comfortable. And then the **4th Regiment Illinois Volunteers** attacked! Santa Anna had to hop for it, leaving his leg (and lunch) behind.

Rest in Pieces Santa Anna

The Illinois soldiers brought the wood-and-cork trophy back with them to **Springfield, Illinois**, and placed it on display in a museum at **Camp Lincoln**. The Mexican government asked for it back several times, but with no luck.

Santa Anna is Spanish for "Saint Anne."

iPuzzle
Lucky 13

Circle every word with one of these objects in front of it:

- star
- red object
- round object
- liverwurst
- triangle
- rat

When you're done, read the circled words (there will be 13 of them) from top to bottom to discover Santa Anna's full name.

ANTONIO	RAÚL	JOSÉ
LA	GARZA	DE
CRUZ	PADUA	SANTA
MARÍA	ANNA	PÉREZ
SEVERINO	Y	MENDEZ
LÓPEZ	FLORES	DELGADO
Y	DE	EL
DE	HIDALGO	SANTA
ANNA	GÓMEZ	RIOS
TACO	Y	CORTES
PÉREZ	XALAPA	NUEVA
SANTA	DE	Y
RIVERA	ANNA	LEBRÓN

Revolving Door: Santa Anna's dashing personality got him elected president 11 different times, but it was never long before he wore out his welcome. Among other things, he overspent, stole money, and lost large amounts of territory to the United States. He became so unpopular in Mexico that he had to live many of his last years in other countries. He returned to Mexico City in 1874, two years before his death.

Jump to this page **or** follow the pipes.

Bathroom Break

We interrupt our historical tour to bring you an important message from your intrepid host, Dwayne the lab rat…

Splutter…gag…cough…gasp…ptooey!

Five Minutes Later…

Okay, sorry about that. I've caught my breath. Traveling through all these sewer pipes is hard work. Moist work, too.

Before we venture back down the drain pipes of history, let's take a moment to find out a bit more about the semi-big brains behind this Interpipe adventure—the Four P's.

Their Other Work

The Four P's have come up with a lot of other toilet-inspired inventions over the years. Why haven't you heard of these products? As you'll see on the next page, they were…well, stinkers (so to speak)!

Near-Miss Inventions from the 4 P's

The Go-Mobile by Plumb Bob: This is basically a toilet on wheels. It runs on gas, but not the kind sold at gas stations. I'll say no more.

Plunger Caps by Phyllis Tanks: Designed to help moms keep track of their kids in shopping malls. The hats came in four colors—classic red, yellow, hot pink, and brown. Offered once on a TV shopping station, only seven were sold, none of them brown.

The Liddy Seat by P. Liddy: Hoping to offer comfort to the backsides of sports fans, Liddy bought a leftover supply of padded toilet seats and repackaged them as stadium cushions. Alas, padded seats that weren't very popular for use in bathrooms were even less popular for use in stadiums.

I-Want-My-Mummy by Portia Potty: A Halloween costume kit that included a roll of toilet paper and a jar of Egyptian dust. Buyers liked the idea of rolling themselves in toilet paper to look like a mummy. They didn't like the idea of paying $29.95 to do it (necessary because of the cost of importing crates of sand and dirt from Egypt).

Okay, Flushing Time!

As we say in the toilet biz—ready, set, GO!

Back to the toilet on the previous page to continue our journey!

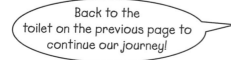

Jump to this page **or** follow the pipes.

1866

It's 5:00 in the morning, and I'm scampering up a cobblestone street in **Blackburn, England**. I'm following a man who's knocking on bedroom windows with a bamboo pole. He's what the people here call…

The Knocker-Up

A row of small two-story houses lines the street. They're all the same, with a kitchen/living room on the first floor, a washroom behind, and two small bedrooms above. All the people living in these houses—men, women, and children—work at the nearby **cotton mill**.

The **knocker-up** works at the mill as well, but he's got an additional job—waking everyone up. Nobody had alarm clocks then, so knocker-ups roamed the streets with their long poles. At the end of the poles, a cluster of metal wires stuck out like a little rake. The knocker-up's "tap, tap, tap" on each window signaled another workday had arrived.

The mills sometimes paid knocker-ups to awaken their employees. Other times, knocker-ups worked on their own, collecting a few pennies from each customer at the end of the week. The price was worth it—the mill gates would close at 6:00 a.m., and any worker not inside would lose a day's pay.

I followed my knocker-up home after he finished his work. He grabbed a bit of breakfast, then headed out to start a second round of window knocking for those with later-starting jobs. Then it's off to work at the mill for him.

Kids at Work

Employees at the Blackburn cotton mills worked long hours, seven days a week—even children. In 1819, working hours for English kids under 16 was limited to 12 hours a day, and those under nine weren't supposed to work at all, but both rules were often ignored. A "half-time system" went into effect in 1844, which set the workday at six and a half hours for kids under 13, leaving three hours a day for school.

iPuzzle
Windoku

house

penny (P)

cotton

pillow

Draw pictures in the empty window panes
so that they follow the rules in the example.

All 4 pictures in each column

All 4 →
pictures in
each row

All 4 →
pictures in
each bold
box

1.

2.

3.

The Shooter-Up: Instead of using a pole, one clever
knocker-up shot dried peas at her customers' windows with a
rubber tube. Her name was Mary Smith, and she worked in
London into the 1930s (yes, knocker-ups were still around then).
Since her pay was only a few pennies a week per customer, do
you suppose she gathered up the peas and reused them?

Year:
1873
Page:
20
Go Return

Jump to this
page **or** follow
the pipes.

Think electric cars are new? Not so. Robert Anderson of Scotland invented one in the 1830s.

1770

I've popped out of a pipe in **Paris, France**, to watch the world's first motor-vehicle accident! It happened when **Nicolas-Joseph Cugnot** was testing his…umm…well, for now let's call it a…

Cugnot goes for a spin →

Steam Mobile

Most people agree that **Karl Benz**, a German engineer, invented the first **automobile** in 1886. But Frenchman Nicolas-Joseph Cugnot built something very much like a **car** over 100 years earlier. It drove on roads under its own power and carried passengers. But it had no name, so history has never been sure what to call it. Car? Tractor? Wagon? Back in Cugnot's day, some people called it a road locomotive.

Whatever it was, it worked…sort of. A large copper **boiler** hung off the front of the vehicle. Steam from the boiler turned a single front wheel, moving the two-and-a-half-ton contraption forward. A ridged iron band around the wheel helped it grip the road.

In its first test, Cugnot's steam mobile averaged a speed of one mph (1.6 kph). It actually chugged along at twice that speed, but Cugnot had to stop every 15 minutes to refill the boiler with water. The vehicle then had to rest an additional 15 minutes before building up enough steam to continue on its journey.

Despite its unimpressive performance, France's minister of war, the **Duke of Choiseul**, approved another test. He wanted to see if Cugnot's vehicle could be used to carry **cannons** and other heavy equipment up hills. In 1771, Cugnot made a second test run, but it ended badly. Unable to control his steam mobile—it had no brakes—Cugnot crashed the vehicle into a wall. By doing so, he came up with a second invention, the automobile accident!

The project was soon scrapped, and in 1801, Cugnot's steam mobile was parked in the **National Conservatory of Arts and Crafts** in Paris. It's still there.

Cugnot drawing by Merrigh and U. Parent, 1886. Devices from the 1903 Sears, Roebuck Catalogue.

iPuzzle
Whazzat?

Can you identify these 19th- and early-20th-century devices?

1. ___ ice cream maker
2. ___ flour sifter
3. ___ portable ink holder
4. ___ toy steam engine

5. ___ cotton planter
6. ___ typing machine
7. ___ clothes washer
8. ___ electric belt

9. ___ music player
10. ___ coffee grinder
11. ___ hearing device
12. ___ hay loader

"Father" of the Car: A Jesuit priest, Ferdinand Verbiest, reportedly designed a steam-powered car while serving as a missionary in China in the 1670s. But Verbiest couldn't hop aboard his invention. According to his book, *Astronomia Europae*, it was a two-foot-long toy.

Year: 1775
Page: 44
Go Return

Jump to this page **or** follow the pipes.

In 1867, Sylvester Roper of America invented a steam motorcycle powered by coal.

1936

Wow, look at all the **bullion** (gold bars) in this room!
And…yikes…guards with guns. Don't shoot!

Billions in Bullion

In the early 1930s, Americans weren't spending their gold; they were hoarding it. That made it difficult for the U.S. government to pay its debts. So two laws were passed requiring most Americans to sell their gold and gold coins to the **U.S. Treasury**. Now the government had a new problem: What to do with this huge new pile of gold?

The answer: build the world's safest vault. In 1936, the **U.S. Mint** put up a building in the middle of **Kentucky** at the **Fort Knox** army base. Its official name was the **U.S. Bullion Depository**, but everyone called it Fort Knox.

The outer walls were four feet thick (1.2 m) and the **vault** door weighed 22 tons. A granite floor ten feet deep (3 m) sat under the building, with layers of concrete beneath that. Ten thousand soldiers, with 300 tanks, trained only a few miles away. Nobody was going to get into this place.

So how'd all that gold get to Fort Knox? The **U.S. Postal Service** delivered it! First, the gold was collected at the **Philadelphia Mint** and the **New York Assay Office**. Then it was melted into bars. Workers loaded the bars on trucks, and motorcycle cops escorted the trucks to awaiting trains. Six billion dollars worth of gold would make the trip (more would be added in later years).

The first shipment went fine, but then disaster struck. Heavy rains caused the Ohio River to overflow, flooding the train tracks all around Fort Knox. The trains couldn't get through, and everything had to be halted. A month later, things had dried out and the gold trains began running again. Altogether, it took six months and 552 train cars to finish the job.

The World's Safest Storage Locker

During World War II, two important documents—the Declaration of Independence and the U.S. Constitution—were stored at Fort Knox. The U.S. government wanted them far away from the Atlantic coast where they might be bombed by German airplanes or submarines.

Fort Knox is located at the intersection of Bullion Boulevard and Gold Vault Road.

FORT KNOX

iPuzzle
Double or Half?

The 1936 price of each item below is either double or half of the price shown.
Make your guesses, then follow the lines to see if you're right.

Double

THE 1936 PRICE WAS

Half

Graffiti: In 1975, the U.S. Mint hired workers to count the gold in Fort Knox, bar by bar. The total count: 36,236 bars worth over $500 billion. But there was a surprise. The gold counters found messages scrawled on the walls behind the gold bars (left by the workers who'd stacked the gold there back in 1936). One said, "Help, I'm trapped in a gold vault."

Jump to this page **or** follow the pipes.

860 I've come to the home of **Duan Chengshi** in China to read his new book. It includes a story that sounds a lot like **Cinderella**!

Cave-Festival Girl

Chengshi called his story *Ye Xian*, named for the girl who stars in it. The people on the south coast of China had been telling it to each other for a long time. Some say Chengshi put the story in his book, *Miscellaneous Morsels from Youyang*, after hearing it from his servant, **Li Shi Yuan**.

How close was it to *Cinderella*? Let's take a quick look at the plot and see.

> Ye Xian's stepmother dressed Ye Xian in rags and gave her all the worst jobs. She was jealous that Ye Xian was smarter and prettier than her own daughter. One day, the stepmother discovered Ye Xian's only friend was a red goldfish. She captured and ate it for dinner. Ye Xian was very sad until an old man came down from the sky to tell her the fish's bones would make Ye Xian's wishes come true.

> Ye Xian used the bones to get a fancy blue feather dress and a pair of shiny golden shoes. She wore them to the Cave Festival and was a big hit. But when her stepmother recognized her, Ye Xian ran off, leaving one shoe behind. The king used the shoe to track her down, and they were married. A shower of rocks then came out of nowhere, killing Ye Xian's stepmother and stepsister.

Aside from the red goldfish and a "rocky" end for the villains, it's a lot like *Cinderella*, isn't it? **Charles Perrault** published that story in 1697, but many people think it was based on this ancient Chinese tale. Some have suggested **Marco Polo** might have brought the story to **Europe** from his travels in **Asia** (see page 10), but nobody really knows. However, Perrault's version added some popular elements: Cinderella's glass slippers, a fairy godmother, and a pumpkin coach that changes back after midnight. Plus—a rat drove the coach! :-)

Around the World

Cinderella-like tales have been told in many countries throughout history, each with its own details. In the Philippines, a girl name Maria is helped by a magical crab. In Germany, one of Aschenputtel's stepsisters cuts off her own toes so her foot will fit in the slipper. Her second stepsister cuts off her heel to squeeze her foot in. Ouch!

An early version of the *Goldilocks* tale starred a fox named Scrapefoot instead of a little girl.

iPuzzle

Name Game

Cinderella goes by different
names in different countries.

6 letters
PELENĖ   [Lithuania]

7 letters
ASKEPOT   [Denmark]
POPELKA   [Czech Republic]
TUHKIMO   [Finland]

8 letters
HIRUSHJA   [Albania]

9 letters
KULKEDISI   [Turkey]
PEPELJUGA   [Croatia]
VENTAFOCS   [Catalonia]

10 letters
CENDRILLON   [France]
CENICIENTA   [Spain]
KOPCIUSZEK   [Poland]

There's only one way to fit
all the names in the puzzle.

When you're done, read the letters
in the highlighted boxes—from
bottom to *top*—to answer this joke:

**Why did Cinderella get
kicked off the soccer team?**

Rhodopis: *Cinderella*-like stories date back to at least
the 1st century B.C. in Greece. The plot: When a girl named
Rhodopis is bathing one day, a falcon grabs one of her sandals,
flies to Egypt, and drops it in the lap of a king. The king sends
his men in search of the sandal's owner. They find Rhodopis,
who then marries the king.

Jump to this
page **or** follow
the pipes.

1966 Yuck! I'm in a storm drain on Wisconsin Avenue in **Washington, D.C.**, and it's pretty mucky. But it gives me a great view of a whiskered, gray-and-white CIA spy coming my way. It's a cat!

Acoustic Kitty

In the early '60s, the **CIA** (the U.S. spy agency) had an idea. Since **cats** can roam freely without attracting attention, how about turning one into a listening device? Enemy spies would never suspect a cat was…a bug.

The project was code-named **Acoustic Kitty** (acoustic means "relating to sound"). The CIA's tech wizards went to work finding tiny sound equipment. An animal doctor then planted the items in a cat—small **batteries** in its belly, a **microphone** in one ear, a **transmitter** at the back of the skull, and a thin **antenna** that ran down the cat's back.

Just one problem: their new spy cat showed more interest in food or squirrels than doing what they wanted it to. The CIA team went back to work. They attached some wires to the cat's brain, hoping they could control the cat that way. Amazingly, it seemed to work (exactly how is top secret).

For the big test, the Acoustic Kitty team drove their van to a nearby park. They released the cat near a bench where two men were talking. To their horror, the cat immediately wandered into the street and was run over by a taxi. Victor Marchetti, a former CIA officer, said, "There they were, sitting in the van with all those dials, and the cat was dead."

The project was soon dead, too. The CIA spent over $15 million and had only a squashed cat to show for it. Still, the official report claimed they'd scored "a remarkable scientific achievement" and concluded that "the work done on this problem over the years reflects great credit on the [people] who guided it."

What's the Latest Poop?

On display at the International Spy Museum in Washington, D.C., is a piece of fake dog doo with a hollow center. Spies would leave their messages inside it, figuring nobody else would touch it.

The CIA tried using mind readers in the 1970s, but with no success.

iPuzzle
Coded Jokes

Write down the first letter of every picture to spell out punch lines.
Then match up the punch lines with the correct jokes at the bottom.

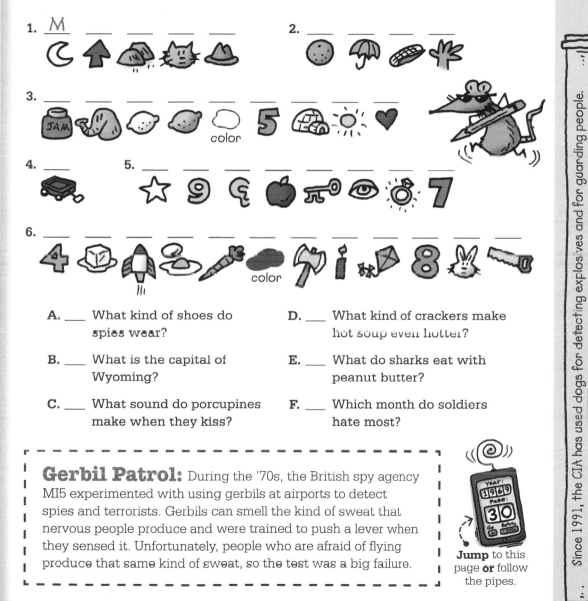

A. ___ What kind of shoes do spies wear?

B. ___ What is the capital of Wyoming?

C. ___ What sound do porcupines make when they kiss?

D. ___ What kind of crackers make hot soup even hotter?

E. ___ What do sharks eat with peanut butter?

F. ___ Which month do soldiers hate most?

Gerbil Patrol: During the '70s, the British spy agency MI5 experimented with using gerbils at airports to detect spies and terrorists. Gerbils can smell the kind of sweat that nervous people produce and were trained to push a lever when they sensed it. Unfortunately, people who are afraid of flying produce that same kind of sweat, so the test was a big failure.

Jump to this page **or** follow the pipes.

Since 1991, the CIA has used dogs for detecting explosives and for guarding people.

1583 I'm making three stops in and around **Copenhagen, Denmark**, because a lot of **amusement-park** history has been made here. Fasten your seat belts. We're in for a fun (and weird) ride!

Forlystelsesparker ←

That means "amusement parks" in Danish.

The World's Oldest: In 1583, a woman named **Kirsten Piil** discovered a pure-water spring in a forest just north of Copenhagen. Crowds started flocking to drink from it, thinking it would cure their ills. If nothing else, the water tasted a lot better than the "eel soup" that flowed in Copenhagen (that's what everyone called the water there).

The area around the spring came to be known as **Bakken**, short for Dyrehavsbakken ("Deer Park Hill"). An unofficial **fair**—with entertainers, food, and things to buy—grew up around it. One man sold clay bowls for drinking the water, then set up defective bowls to be knocked down for a price—the park's first arcade game! Over the years, tents were added, then music halls, and finally rides. The amusement park attracts over two million visitors a year. The spring? It dried out long ago!

The World's Second Oldest: In 1843, **Tivoli Gardens** opened in Copenhagen. Its founder convinced the king of Denmark to let him build it by saying, "When the people are amusing themselves, they do not think about politics." The park is a beautiful mix of rides, buildings, and gardens, much of it with an Asian theme. ──→ Because of that, some people say it's the world's first **theme park**.

Photo by Malte Hübner

The World's Weirdest: BonBon-Land opened in a small town southwest of Copenhagen in 1992. Its inspiration came from the BonBon candy company, maker of sweets with names such as Sea Gull Droppings, Boogers, Dead Flies, Earwax, and Dog Farts.

BonBon-Land's strangest roller coaster is called **The Farting Dog**. Visitors are greeted by a large sculpture of **Henry Hound** standing amid piles of poop. The ride itself travels through a dog house that plays farting noises. Among the other artwork at BonBon-Land: a vomiting rat, a peeing ant, and a sea gull pooping into an alligator's mouth.

"Adventure" is the most common word used in amusement-park names.

iPuzzle
Amusing Parks

Four of these amusement parks actually exist. Two don't. Write
REAL or FAKE in each blank, then do the math to find out if you're
right. If the answer is UNDER 10 = REAL. If it's OVER 10 = FAKE.

1. _____ *Santa Claus Land* in Indiana. Its attractions
have included Blitzen's Airplanes, Dasher's Seahorses,
and a water-ski thrill show performed on Lake Rudolph.

$5 \times 3 - 7 + 1 =$ _____

2. _____ *Republic of the Children* in Argentina features
a kid-size city where visitors can take out pretend bank
loans, pass laws, and visit an underground prison.

$2 + 7 \div 3 + 5 =$ _____

3 _____ *Whoop-di-doo Animal Park* in Cuba offers
giraffe rides, a pool for swimming with walruses, and
what the park claims is a real unicorn.

$3 + 4 \times 2 - 2 =$ _____

4. _____ *Shijingshan Amusement Park* in China features
rip-off Disney buildings and characters, including a Minnie
Mouse look-alike the park insists is a cat with large ears.

$6 \cdot 3 \times 4 - 3 =$ _____

5. _____ *Mukluk Land* in Alaska boasts the world's
largest mukluk (an arctic boot) and largest mosquito, a
display of old snowmobiles, and Skee-Ball games.

$9 + 6 \div 5 + 4 =$ _____

6. _____ *Crocodile Nigeria*. Visitors can canoe through
crocodile swamps or walk on rickety bridges overhead to
feed the crocs chunks of red meat at 3:00 p.m. every day.

$5 \times 4 \div 2 + 1 =$ _____

On Your Own ⟶

Do-it-yourself
instructions
for one of the
smaller rides at
BonBon-Land.
Really!

Instructions

Passenger: *Get in and close strap!*

Waiting person: 1. *Please close door <u>from outside!</u>*
2. *When lamp green, press button!*

Passenger: *Press the start button — Go ahead.*

*After the ride, when the gate opens, press
the release button and open the strap.*

Jump to this
page **or** follow
the pipes.

Merry-go-rounds were invented in the 160Cs for teaching French noblemen how to ride horses. ...

1974 You'll never believe who I found here on the **Philippine** island of **Lubang**. **Hiroo Onoda**, a Japanese army officer who has been hiding here for 29 years. Why? He doesn't know **World War II** ended in 1945!

One-Man War

Lubang Island

Not long after Japan entered World War II, Hiroo Onoda joined the army. He received training as an **intelligence officer**, and on New Year's Eve 1944, took over as the leader of a small group of men on Lubang.

Before Onoda left for the island, a general told him, "It may take three years, it may take five, but whatever happens, we'll come back for you. Until then, as long as you have one soldier, you are to continue to lead him."

Just two months after Onoda's arrival, an American ship docked at the island. At the time, more than one hundred Japanese troops were stationed there. The Americans killed or captured all but Onoda and three other men. The foursome hid out in the jungle, keeping on the move to avoid being found.

After the war ended in August 1945, airplanes dropped leaflets on Lubang announcing the news. "A trick by the enemy," Onoda's group concluded. More leaflets followed over the years, in addition to newspapers, letters, and photos from home. Soldiers who'd surrendered left notes reading, "Nobody is searching for you now but Japanese. Come on out!" All fakes, the foursome said.

Onoda's group slowly shrank. In 1949, one of them surrendered. In 1954, another was killed in a shoot-out with a search party he thought was the enemy. In 1972, the last of Onoda's companions was shot while stealing rice. He soon died.

In 1974, a college dropout named **Norio Suzuki** went on a quest to find Hiroo Onoda. Many people thought Onoda didn't exist—he was officially listed as dead in 1959—but Suzuki found him. Convincing him to leave the island was another thing. Onoda's former commander, now a bookseller, had to be flown to the island to give the orders in person.

Hiroo Onoda arrived back home 29 years after he'd left, hailed as a hero for his loyalty and for never giving up.

iPuzzle
Character Count

Each character (in blue) appears a different number of times—except for two of the characters, which appear the exact same number of times. Find those two.

SUPER-EXTRA CREDIT: There are 42 blue characters. Before counting the characters individually, can you figure out what the count will be for the two characters that appear the exact same number of times?

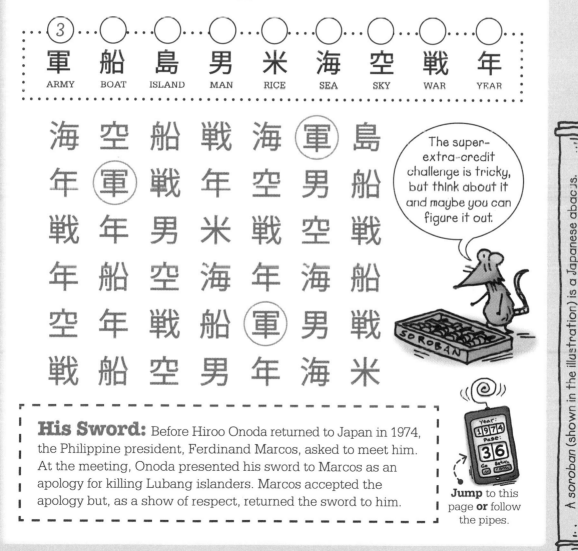

③ ◯ ◯ ◯ ◯ ◯ ◯ ◯ ◯

軍	船	島	男	米	海	空	戦	年
ARMY	BOAT	ISLAND	MAN	RICE	SEA	SKY	WAR	YEAR

海 空 船 戦 海 軍 島
年 軍 戦 年 空 男 船
戦 年 男 米 戦 空 戦
年 船 空 海 年 海 船
空 年 戦 船 軍 男 戦
戦 船 空 男 年 海 米

> The super-extra-credit challenge is tricky, but think about it and maybe you can figure it out.

SOROBAN

His Sword: Before Hiroo Onoda returned to Japan in 1974, the Philippine president, Ferdinand Marcos, asked to meet him. At the meeting, Onoda presented his sword to Marcos as an apology for killing Lubang islanders. Marcos accepted the apology but, as a show of respect, returned the sword to him.

Year: 1974
Page: 36
Go Return

Jump to this page **or** follow the pipes.

A soroban (shown in the illustration) is a Japanese abacus.

1960 I'm at **Cape Canaveral** in **Florida**, where the **U.S. Navy** has just launched a rocket. It was supposed to go into space, but it's heading for a cow in **Cuba**.

Duck, Cow!

The **Thor DM-21 rocket** was designed to deliver a **satellite** into orbit to provide positioning information to Navy ships and subs. But the rocket veered off course and broke into pieces over Cuba, about 375 miles (600 km) south of Cape Canaveral.

Up until 1959, this might not have been too much of a problem. The U.S. and Cuba had a friendly enough relationship. But that changed with the 1959 **Cuban Revolution**, led by **Fidel Castro.** Castro took control of the country and, along with it, some U.S.-owned companies within its borders. He also heavily taxed U.S. imports. That didn't go over well with the American companies involved or the **U.S. President**, **Dwight David Eisenhower.**

All ties between the two countries broke off, and neither of them missed an opportunity to complain about the other's behavior. So when the Navy rocket went kablooey, Castro immediately responded. Here's the way **CIA Director David Tennet** described the incident in 2000:

> "One of (the) more spectacular failures rained debris down on Cuba. Havana charged that a cow was killed in a deliberate U.S. action. The Cubans soon paraded another cow through the streets with a placard reading 'Eisenhower, you murdered one of my sisters.' It was the first and last time that a satellite has been used in the production of ground beef."

Gulp.

The cow was reportedly given a state funeral as the victim of an American attack. Additionally, Castro filed a complaint with the **United Nations**, but nothing came of it. U.S. officials merely laughed it off. Playing off the phrase "the shot heard 'round the world," they referred to the unfortunate accident as "the herd shot 'round the world."

The U.S. offered Spain $100 million for Cuba in 1848 but was turned down.

iPuzzle
'60 Questions

Match up these questions and answers about things that happened in the year 1960. I'm betting you can do it even if you don't know the answers.

A. Rome   **B.** Chatty Cathy   **C.** *Green Eggs and Ham*   **D.** 179 million
E. Brasília   **F.** Bandaranaike   **G.** *Scent of Mystery*   **H.** 70 million

1. ___ What movie opened, using Smell-O-Vision for the first and only time in theaters? ← *30 odors came from under the chairs.*

2. ___ What was the U.S. population, according to the 1960 U.S. Census count? ← *The total is rounded off.*

3. ___ What city replaced Rio de Janeiro as the capital of a South American country? ← *The city was built in 41 months, just for that purpose.*

4. ___ How many people watched the first ever televised presidential debate between Kennedy and Nixon? ← *Also rounded off.*

5. ___ In what city was the Summer Olympics held?

6. ___ What doll debuted, capable of saying phrases such as "Please take me with you" when a string was pulled?

7. ___ What Dr. Seuss book was released in August?

8. ___ What was the last name of Ceylon's (Sri Lanka) new prime minister, the world's first female prime minister?

Stuck in the '50s: Soon after the 1959 Cuban Revolution, the U.S. prohibited American cars from being sold in Cuba. So Cubans just kept repairing the ones they already had. Today, there are an estimated 60,000 American cars built before 1960 roaming the streets of Cuba. The locals call them "Yank tanks" (Yank being a nickname for an American).

Year: 1966
Page: 58
Go Return

Jump to this page **or** follow the pipes.

Government officials in Cuba are required to pick up hitchhikers.

Cubans call their island *El Cocodrilo* (crocodile) because it's shaped like a crocodile.

46 B.C. It took me a couple of tries to get to **Rome** on this exact date. That's because **Emperor Julius Caesar** has been monkeying with time. This year alone, he threw three extra months into the calendar, making the year 445 days long!

Year of Confusion

I think of a year as being 365 days long. Everyone does, right? Not in ancient Rome. The Romans measured their months using the **Moon**…sort of. The length of time between new moons is about 29 and a half days. The **Roman calendar** started with that, but eventually ended up with seven 29-day months, five 31-day months, and one 28-day month—February. The problem was that the total number of days added up to only 355—10 days short of a full year.

Pretty soon, spring arrived in the winter and autumn during the summer. The Romans weren't dummies; they realized they shouldn't be having a **harvest festival** when their crops had just been planted. So Julius Caesar ordered up a new calendar.

Sosigenes, a Greek astronomer living in **Egypt**, told Caesar a year lasted 365.25 days. Based on that, Caesar lengthened most of the months by one or two days, for a total of 365 days. A leap day was added to February every fourth year.

Caesar's new creation, called the **Julian Calendar**, would go into effect in 45 B.C., but first, some repair work had to be done. The old calendar had allowed the year to creep backward by 80 days!

In 46 B.C., Caesar added an extra month after February and shoehorned two more months between November and December. Because of that, 46 B.C. would later be called "**the year of confusion**." But by the time 45 B.C. *finally* rolled around, all the days were back where they belonged. January 1 was taking place toward the beginning of winter instead of the beginning of autumn. Most of **Europe** soon adopted the Julian Calendar, which is pretty much the same one used today.

Friends
Romans
Country-men

THIS YEAR'S LINE·UP

JANUARIS
FEBRUARIS
NEW!
MERCE-DONIUS
MARTIUS
APRILIS
MAIUS
JUNIUS
QUINTILIS
SEXTILIS
SEPTEMBER
OCTOBER
NOVEMBER
NEW!
INTERCALARIS PRIOR & POSTERIOR
DECEMBER

In 46 B.C., Romans called the year 708 a.u.c. (*ab urbe condita*, "after the birth of Rome").

iPuzzle
Calendar Jokes

Match the correct punch line to each joke.

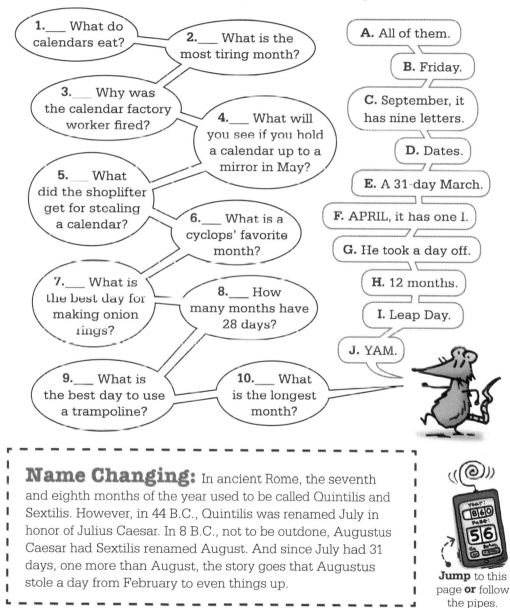

1.___ What do calendars eat?

2.___ What is the most tiring month?

3.___ Why was the calendar factory worker fired?

4.___ What will you see if you hold a calendar up to a mirror in May?

5.___ What did the shoplifter get for stealing a calendar?

6.___ What is a cyclops' favorite month?

7.___ What is the best day for making onion rings?

8.___ How many months have 28 days?

9.___ What is the best day to use a trampoline?

10.___ What is the longest month?

A. All of them.

B. Friday.

C. September, it has nine letters.

D. Dates.

E. A 31-day March.

F. APRIL, it has one I.

G. He took a day off.

H. 12 months.

I. Leap Day.

J. YAM.

Name Changing: In ancient Rome, the seventh and eighth months of the year used to be called Quintilis and Sextilis. However, in 44 B.C., Quintilis was renamed July in honor of Julius Caesar. In 8 B.C., not to be outdone, Augustus Caesar had Sextilis renamed August. And since July had 31 days, one more than August, the story goes that Augustus stole a day from February to even things up.

Jump to this page **or** follow the pipes.

In 1582, the Gregorian calendar made a few final adjustments to the Julian calendar.

1913 It's a cold December 21st morning, and I'm wandering the streets of **New York City** to get a copy of the Sunday *New York World* newspaper. Inside it is the world's first **crossword puzzle**, a creation that will become a national craze.

Puzzle Mania

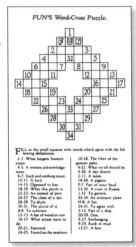

The first crossword

Arthur Wynne edited an eight-page "Fun" section each week for the Sunday *New York World*. It included riddles, math puzzles, cartoons, and other amusements. One week, Wynne's editor asked if he could come up with a new type of puzzle for the section. Wynne's diamond-shaped puzzle of crisscrossing words was the result. He called it a Word-Cross puzzle, although the name would soon be changed to Cross-Word and eventually just crossword.

Readers loved the puzzle so much, they complained if one didn't appear each week. They also complained about the many mistakes they found, so the paper hired a young assistant, **Margaret Petherbridge**. Petherbridge tightened things up and took over as editor when Wynne retired. Her careful (and fun) style made the puzzles even more popular.

In 1924, Petherbridge helped edit **Simon & Schuster**'s first-ever book, a collection of crossword puzzles. The book immediately sold out, and a nationwide crossword craze soon followed. The **B&O Railroad** offered **dictionaries** on its trains to help crossword-solving riders. The **New York Public Library** had to limit use of reference books to five minutes in an attempt to keep the waiting line of "puzzle fans" from growing too long.

Companies started making crossword-themed merchandise of every sort—clothing, jewelry, even a tiny dictionary on a wrist band. There were songs, such as "**Cross Words Between Sweetie and Me**" and a Broadway musical revue titled *Puzzles of 1925*.

My favorite was a seven-minute Disney **animated film** called *Alice Solves the Puzzle*. In it, a real-life girl named Alice shares the screen with a cartoon cat named **Julius** and **Bootleg Pete**, a bearlike collector of rare crossword puzzles.

Brrr

iPuzzle
Wynne Win

All the words from the world's first crossword puzzle are listed below.
Work off of the ones already entered in the diagram to fill in the others.
There's only one way they'll all fit. No guessing is required!

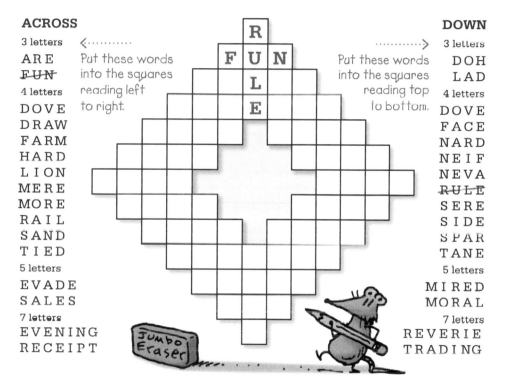

ACROSS

3 letters ← · · · · · · · · · ·

ARE

~~FUN~~

4 letters

DOVE

DRAW

FARM

HARD

LION

MERE

MORE

RAIL

SAND

TIED

5 letters

EVADE

SALES

7 letters

EVENING

RECEIPT

Put these words into the squares reading left to right.

Put these words into the squares reading top to bottom.

· · · · · · · · · · ·>

DOWN

3 letters

DOH

LAD

4 letters

DOVE

FACE

NARD

NEIF

NEVA

~~RULE~~

SERE

SIDE

SPAR

TANE

5 letters

MIRED

MORAL

7 letters

REVERIE

TRADING

EXTRA CREDIT: Did you notice DOVE appears twice? That wouldn't be allowed today.
Changing one letter in one DOVE, can you fix it so it makes a new word both ways?

Crosswordese is what people call little-known words
that appear in crossword puzzles but hardly anywhere else. The
crossword puzzle above is a good example. Here are five words
from it, followed by the definitions given for them: NEIF—part
of a ship • TANE—one • NEVA—a river in Russia • NARD—an
aromatic plant • DOH—the fibre of the gomuti palm.

Jump to this
page **or** follow
the pipes.

In 1959, the Williams company put out a Crossword pinball game.

1861 I've scampered up a hillside in **Centreville, Virginia**. It's a warm Sunday afternoon in July, and the hill is full of men and women with picnic baskets and...binoculars. What are they watching? The first major land battle of the **American Civil War**.

Battle and a Bite

In the days before this battle, known as the **Battle of Bull Run**, people in nearby **Washington, D.C.**, could talk of little else. They all expected a huge victory for the North and, possibly, a quick end to the war.

When the day of the battle arrived, spectators on horseback and in carriages filled the roads leading to Centreville. The high ground there provided a sweeping view of the battlefield five miles away. The crowd, about 500 strong, included politicians, reporters, workers who had the day off, and the occasional "huckster" selling pies and snacks to those who hadn't thought to pack a lunch.

Unfortunately, when the fighting began, nobody could see much. Thick woods covered the ground below. The noise and white smoke of rifle and cannon fire provided the only evidence of a battle. As to what was actually happening, the onlookers could only guess.

A group of about 50 politicians and reporters, itching for something more than a view of the surrounding treetops, moved closer. They ended up on a ridge only a mile from the action. The scene that soon unfolded didn't match the visions of victory they had expected. Strengthened by fresh troops, the South took control of the fight, forcing the North to retreat. The withdrawal quickly turned into a panicked stampede of soldiers, horses, and wagons. Amid the confusion, one Congressman was taken prisoner.

Word of the disaster soon filtered back to the tree-watching picnickers in Centreville. They quickly packed up their things and fled, filling the roads back to Washington.

The "quick end" to the war that many in Washington seemed sure of would take four long and deadly years.

iPuzzle
Scenes at a Picnic

Write numbers in the circles to show the order
in which items were removed from the basket.

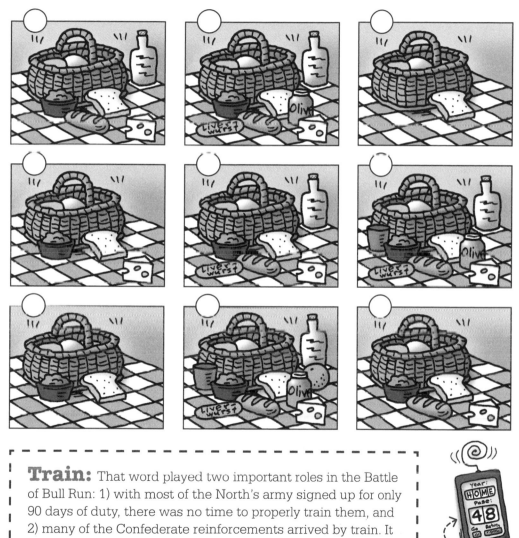

Train: That word played two important roles in the Battle of Bull Run: 1) with most of the North's army signed up for only 90 days of duty, there was no time to properly train them, and 2) many of the Confederate reinforcements arrived by train. It was the first battle in American history where that was done. Railroads would be used extensively throughout the war.

Year: HOME Page: **48** Go Return

Jump to this page **or** follow the pipes.

1876 I've traveled to the **Amazon rain forest** in **Brazil**, home of the only **rubber trees** on the planet. But that's about to change, thanks to Englishman **Henry Wickham**, a failed farmer turned...

Rubber Robber

A rubber seed, actual size →

Tapping a rubber tree

In 1839, **Charles Goodyear** invented **vulcanized rubber** by mixing **sulfur** with raw rubber. That was a big deal because ordinary rubber became sticky and stinky in hot weather and brittle in the cold. Goodyear's new wonder material had all sorts of uses: hoses, tires, balls, electrical-wire coating, raincoats, boots, rubber bands, gloves, even a new jawbone for Grover Cleveland (see page 40).

Just one problem: Brazil had the world's only supply of raw rubber—it had a **monopoly**. The British in particular didn't like that. So they set about trying to get some seeds of their own to grow rubber trees in lands they controlled. Easier said than done.

In 1850, British plant expert **Richard Spruce** landed in Brazil. He found some rubber seeds, but they all rotted on the trip to London. In 1873, **Charles Ferris** gathered 2,000 seeds and shipped them hidden inside two stuffed crocodiles. They rotted, too. Two years later, **Ricardo Chávez** sent 500 lbs. of rubber seeds. Some of them might have survived the trip to London, but we'll never know. A bumbling clerk accidentally forwarded them to **India**, dooming the whole load.

Success came in 1876 from an unexpected source. Henry Wickham, a "traveling artist" living in **Santarém, Brazil**, had failed at almost everything he'd tried. But he'd come to know the rubber tree, a rare claim for a non-Brazilian. That spring, Wickham worked nonstop gathering and buying only the best seeds, bringing in an incredible haul of 70,000. He carefully packed them between layers of dried **banana leaves** and escorted them back to London himself aboard the SS *Amazonas*. His shipment of seeds weighed a ton and a half.

Enough seeds survived to grow 2,700 trees in London's **Kew Gardens**. And within 34 years, British rubber plantations in the **Far East** flooded the market with cheap rubber, wiping out Brazil's monopoly for good.

Photos: Rubber tree by Iamshibuka; rubber seed by Luis Fernández García.

Rubber was first brought to Europe in 1735 by Frenchman Charles Marie de La Condamine.

Today, around 90 percent of rubber comes from Southeast Asia.

iPuzzle
Monopoly

A professional typist would type MONOPOLY using only the right hand (using the touch-typing method). Similarly, each answer below would be typed using only the left *or* only the right hand. You'll have to figure out which.

LEFT HAND

Q W E R T
A S D F G
Z X C V B

RIGHT HAND

Y U I O P
H J K L
N M

1. Rubber is tapped from them: __ __ __ __ __ ⟵·········• These answers can be found on page 72. •

2. Pig's sound: __ __ __ __

3. Dam-building animal: __ __ __ __ __ __

4. Henry Wickham collected 70,000 of them in Brazil: __ __ __ __ __ ⟵

5. Santa's laugh: __ __ __ __ __ __

6. Black-and-white African animal: __ __ __ __ __

7. Old "wrapped-up" Egyptian: __ __ __ __ __

8. A month: __ __ __ __

9. Compass direction: __ __ __ __ or __ __ __ __ __

10. Halloween vegetable: __ __ __ __ __ __

11. Witch's animal: __ __ __ or __ __ __ or __ __ __

12. Luke Skywalker movie series: __ __ __ __ __ __ __ __

13. 1,000 x 1,000: __ __ __ __ __ __ __

I'm in one of the answers!

EXTRA CREDIT: Can you come up with a…

…boy's first name using the left hand? _____

…girl's first name using the left hand? _____

…boy's first name using the right hand? _____

…girl's first name using the right hand? _____

Year: 1888
Page: 28
Go Return

Jump to this page **or** follow the pipes.

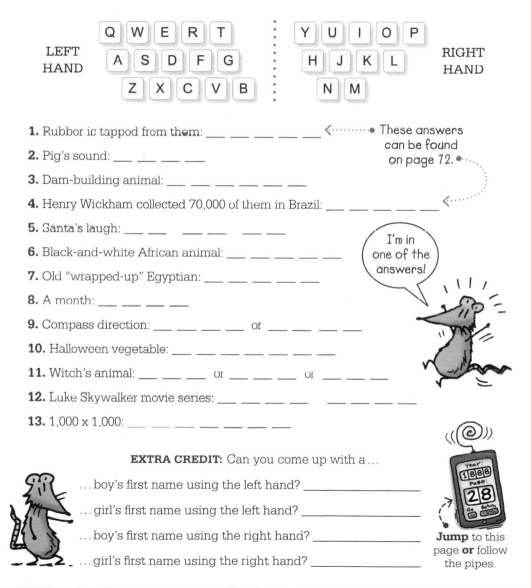

Photo by Riba.

1902

It's cramped and stuffy in this stone jail in **Saint-Pierre**, the capital of **Martinique** in the Caribbean. But for the jail's one prisoner, August Cyparis, it's about to become the safest spot in town.

Crime Pays

The jail in ⟶
Saint-Pierre

In early 1902, **Mount Pelée**, a sleeping **volcano** sitting above Saint-Pierre woke up. It started spewing out bits of ash and sulfuric gas. The insects and snakes that lived on its slopes knew enough to flee. But Martinique's governor, **Louis Mouttet**, didn't. Based on an inspection of the volcano by the high school's science teacher, Mouttet assured everyone in Saint-Pierre that the growling mountain posed no danger.

But he had an extra reason for wanting to say that: An important **election** approached, and the governor didn't want any residents to leave, especially his wealthy supporters. He needed their votes!

August Cyparis couldn't have gone anywhere if he'd wanted to. He'd been thrown in jail on May 7 for taking part in a drunken brawl. The one-room jail was windowless and bomb-proof, originally used to store ammunition. As it turned out, being locked inside it was the best thing that could have happened to Cyparis.

The next morning, Mount Pelée blew its top. A glowing cloud of poisonous gas, steam, and scorchingly hot ash and rock (a *nuée ardente*) raced down the mountain at 400 mph (600 kph). In less than two minutes, the entire town of Saint-Pierre was flattened, its splintered wreckage in flames.

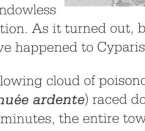

Of the 28,000 people in the town, Cyparis was the only one still alive. Two others had escaped, one by land and one by sea, while thousands died elsewhere on the island. Four days later, workers found Cyparis in the jail amid the smoldering rubble. His back was burned from hot air and ashes that had seeped through a slit in the jailhouse door, but otherwise he was unharmed.

iPuzzle

Volcano Search

Look for each volcano term reading either left, right, up, down or diagonally.

- ACTIVE
- ASHES
- CLOUD
- CONE
- CRATER
- DORMANT
- ERUPTION
- FLOW
- LAVA
- MAGMA
- MANTLE
- MOLTEN
- PUMICE
- SPEW
- TREMOR
- TRENCH
- VENT

I	S	R	E	T	A	R	C	R	C	I	D
S	D	B	W	H	R	S	V	T	A	B	H
Y	S	M	O	L	T	E	N	O	C	K	B
U	C	P	A	R	N	H	M	T	U	O	U
E	A	V	E	T	D	S	N	O	E	L	L
F	A	N	W	W	Z	A	G	U	R	P	Z
P	C	M	A	G	M	A	E	Y	U	P	N
H	O	K	R	R	Q	C	V	M	P	W	J
O	X	D	O	J	H	E	I	K	T	K	F
A	N	D	B	O	Q	C	T	L	I	L	E
M	A	N	T	L	E	C	C	L	O	U	D
J	E	H	N	E	K	G	A	W	N	I	D

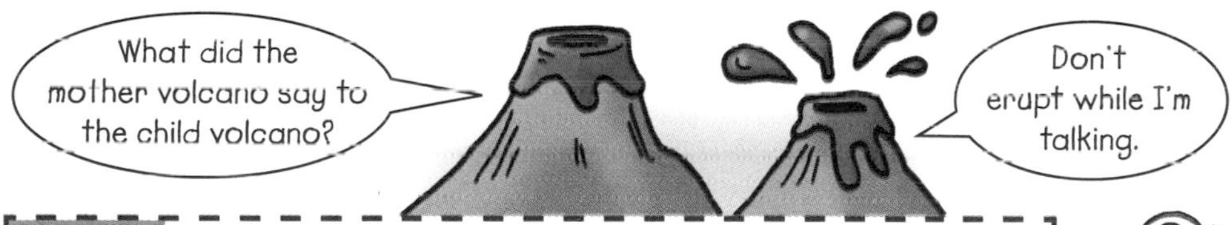

What did the mother volcano say to the child volcano?
Don't erupt while I'm talking.

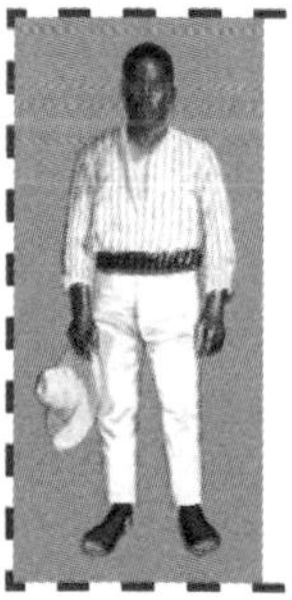

Circus Life: After surviving Mount Pelée's 1902 eruption, August Cyparis toured with the Barnum & Bailey circus. Using the stage name Ludger Sylbaris, he spoke to audiences about being in "the Silent City of Death where 40,000 human beings were suffocated, burned, or buried by one belching blast of Mount Pelée's terrible volcanic eruption."

Year:
1904
Page:
12

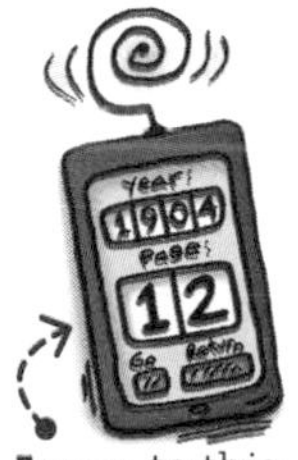

Jump to this page **or** follow the pipes.

Pumice, a type of volcanic rock, can float in water.

Jupiter's Moon, Io, is covered with erupting volcanoes.

1812 Did you know that **Russia** once colonized **northern California**? I'm here to check that out.

Russian America

Ross Colony as drawn by Duhaut-Cilly in 1828

In 1799, Russian Tsar **Paul I** created the **Russian-American Company**. Operating out of Alaska, it would control all Russian trade, exploration, and settlement in North America.

The company was most interested in **sea otters**. The furry mammals thrived along Alaska's coast and the Russians prized their thick fur. But soon after arriving in Alaska, the company had a big problem: how to feed all the workers. They needed fruit, vegetables, and grain—hard things to grow there.

Russian-American Company flag

The company sent an expedition south to search for a place to raise crops. The explorers found a nice spot just north of **San Francisco**, and 95 Russians and 80 native Alaskans started a settlement there. They called it **Ross Colony**. The colonists planted fruit trees and fields of wheat and barley. They traded tools for food with the **Spanish**. They also hunted sea otters along the coast.

Unfortunately, things never worked out as well as the company had hoped. Few of the colonists were farmers, and not many were willing to work in the fields for low pay. On top of that, clammy weather, bad soil, and hungry varmints such as **mice** and **gophers** kept their harvests low. Ross Colony couldn't do much more than feed itself, and the company lost money every year.

In 1841, the Russians finally gave up and sold the 59 buildings of Ross Colony to a Swiss pioneer named **John Sutter** for $30,000. Twenty-six years later, the Russian-American Company called it quits in Alaska as well, selling the land to the U.S. for $7,200,000.

Yum, this Russian wheat is tasty.

Sea otters have one million hairs per square inch.

iPuzzle
Russian Around

The names of 10 Russian settlements have been scrambled to make wacky anagrams (all the same letters in a different order). The real names are listed below. Can you match them up?

Don't miss the one in Hawaii below.

Russia

A. STOMACH LIFTER

B. LO, A NUT!

Alaska

F. ATTACK ONLY YOU

Canada

C. FLIP SOLID BRAINS

G. CHANNEL WAGER

E. KOALA DID SINK

H. FROSTY SUN IDIOTS

D. ANNUAL IDEALISTS

Russian settlement locations:

1. ___ ALEUTIAN ISLANDS
2. ___ FORT ELIZABETH
3. ___ FORT ST. DIONYSIUS
4. ___ FORT ST. MICHAEL
5. ___ KODIAK ISLAND

6. ___ NEW ARCHANGEL
7. ___ NULATO
8. ___ PRIBILOF ISLANDS
9. ___ ROSS COLONY
10. ___ YAKUTAT COLONY

United States

I. LOONY CROSS

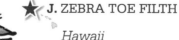

The Russians were in Hawaii in 1817.

J. ZEBRA TOE FILTH

Hawaii

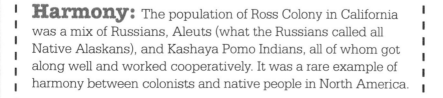

Harmony: The population of Ross Colony in California was a mix of Russians, Aleuts (what the Russians called all Native Alaskans), and Kashaya Pomo Indians, all of whom got along well and worked cooperatively. It was a rare example of harmony between colonists and native people in North America.

Jump to this page **or** follow the pipes.

Year: 1842 Page: 46 Go Return

During the 19th century, the Russian Empire controlled 15 percent of the world's land area.

2005 I've scampered up to the top of a **lighthouse** on the island of **Ushant, France**. And here comes Britain's **Ellen MacArthur** in an attempt to set a speed record for sailing nonstop around the world...alone.

Globe-Sailing

Circling the world in a ship has a long history. **Ferdinand Magellan** was the first to try, in 1519. His expedition required five ships, 270 men, and three years. Philippine warriors killed Magellan halfway through, but in 1522 **Juan Sebastián del Cano** and 17 men completed the journey in the only surviving ship, *Victoria*.

In 1898, **Joshua Slocum** became the first person to sail around the world alone. It took three years and two months aboard a wooden fishing boat named *Spray*.

In 1960, the U.S. Navy's atomic submarine **USS** *Triton* retraced Magellan's route—traveling entirely underwater. The operation was so secret the crew wasn't told what was going on until the sub was two days out of port. The trip took 60 days, 21 hours—two months underwater!

Ellen MacArthur departed in her sailboat, the *B&Q*, from Ushant, France, in late 2004. She headed south in the **Atlantic**, then east around the tip of **Africa**.

That's when the most dangerous part of her journey began. The **Southern Ocean**, just north of **Antarctica**, is home to huge waves, storm-force winds, freezing weather, and icebergs. "I have never had to dig that deep in my life," MacArthur said about the miserable conditions she faced for well over a month. The only rest she got? Ten half-hour naps per day.

MacArthur had an entirely different problem after rounding the tip of **South America**. The winds died, and she spent five days bobbing in the water. Then, when the breezes did return, she nearly collided with a **whale**. Despite the challenges, she broke the previous record by more than a day. Her time: 71 days, 14 hours.

iPuzzle
Size Them Up

We've drawn these around-the-word ships about the same size—but they're not! Try numbering them in order of how LONG you think they actually are, from shortest to longest. Then follow the lines to see if you're right.

___ USS *Triton* submarine

___ *Earthrace* trimaran speedboat

___ RMS *Laconia* ocean liner

_3_ B&Q trimaran

___ *Victoria* carrack

___ *Spray* yawl

| 1. 40 feet (12 m) | 2. 65 feet (20 m) | 3. 75 feet (23 m) | 4. 78 feet (24 m) | 5. 447 feet (136 m) | 6. 601 feet (183 m) |

Sailing Nut: Ellen MacArthur fell in love with sailing at age four, the first time her aunt took her out on the water. Four years later, she started saving birthday and Christmas money to buy her own boat. In high school, she was given food money each day, but she bought the cheapest possible meal and saved the rest. With her savings, she first bought an 8-foot dinghy and then, at age 17, a 21-foot yacht with a small cabin.

Jump to this page **or** follow the pipes.

In 1923, the *Laconia* became the first ocean liner to complete an around-the-world cruise. It took 130 days.

1255

Welcome to **San Gimignano, Italy**. The village has just passed a law making it illegal to build anything taller than the city's **Rognosa Tower** (167 feet, 51 m). Will the town's most powerful families obey?

Tower Power

San Gimignano is famous for its towers. Today, 14 of them rise above the *piazze* (plazas) and *palazzi* (grand houses), but there used to be more than 70. Why so many? The answer: a **feud**.

Starting in 1246 and lasting for about 100 years, two families, the **Salvucci** and **Ardinghelli**, battled for control of the town. And we're not talking about running for office and calling each other names. Things got bloody.

The many towers that started to fill the city served as a visible sign of the rivalry. The size of a structure symbolized the importance of the person who built it. It also created a perch for keeping an eye on the enemy and for shooting arrows or dropping boiling oil on them. Other wealthy families, allied with one side or the other, joined in on the building (and fighting) craze as well.

In 1255, the town tried to slow things down by setting a building-height limit. Neither side paid any attention. The Salvucci soon put up a pair of towers that rose above the Rognosa Tower. In response, the Ardinghelli built their own pair of towers directly across the piazza from the Salvucci towers.

The feud finally came to an end in 1353. The town's population had been cut in half by the **Black Death**, a plague sweeping across Europe. On top of that, **Florence**, a powerful city nearby, had become involved in San Gimignano's constant fighting. Florence voted to take control of San Gimignano, with the proposal passing by only one black bean (yes, they voted with beans). Many of the towers were soon lowered or taken down. Others crumbled over the years, leaving just 14.

Because of all its old towers, San Gimignano has been nicknamed the medieval Manhattan.

Photo by Bjørn Christian Tørrissen.

San Gimignano's towers were built for defense, with few windows and narrow doorways.

iPuzzle
Tallest Tower

Which tower of blocks (marked with a number) rises highest above the floor? Which is shortest?

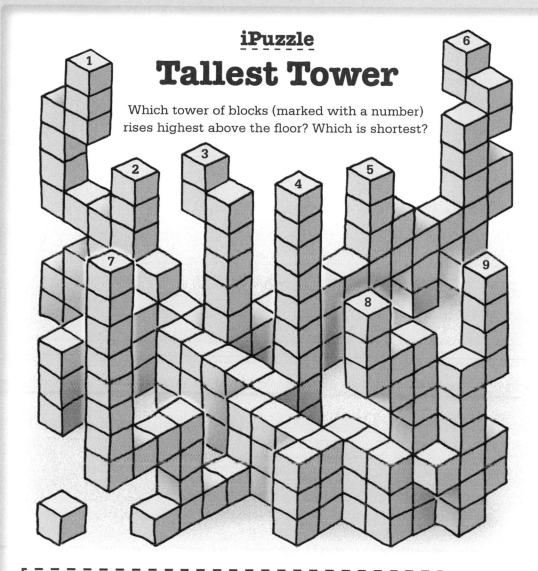

Voting: San Gimignano, Italy, used to have an unusual method for electing a town leader. First, a council picked eight candidates. Next, two tickets, each listing four of the finalists, were sealed in wax and put in a jar of water. A kid reached into the jar and selected one list. The four names on it would then be written on four separate tickets, each sealed in wax and placed in the water jar. The kid would select one of the four tickets—the winner.

Jump to this page **or** follow the pipes.

1545 Grab a gourd and start bailing water! There are fabulous riches to be found in **Lake Guatavita** in **Colombia**. At least that's what I hear these Spanish **conquistadors** (explorers and soldiers) saying.

Lagoon of Gold

Soon after the Spanish came to **South America**, the legend of a lost city of gold captured their imaginations. It appears to have come from stories the **Muisca** people told of a "Golden Man" (**El Dorado** in Spanish).

After the Muisca appointed a new **Zipa** (ruler), a ceremony took place on Lake Guatavita. A decorated **raft** with a pot of **incense** at each corner carried the Zipa and his attendants to the middle of the lake. All wore fancy plumes and golden jewelry—except for the Zipa. He would be coated head to toe with sticky mud, then covered in gold dust. Each person on the raft made an offering to the Muisca water god by throwing piles of **gold**, **emeralds**, and other treasure overboard.

To the Muisca, gold and jewels had no value other than as gifts to the gods. Not so for the Spanish—they wanted that money! So they devised ways to try to get at the vast riches they thought lay at the bottom of Lake Guatavita.

Lázaro Fonte and **Hernán Perez de Quesada** tried first, in 1545. A line of workers armed with gourd jars managed to lower the water level by 10 feet (3 m) and recovered about $100,000 of gold (in today's money). In 1580, **Antonio de Sepúlveda** cut a huge notch at one end of the lake, lowering the water level by 65 feet (20 m). When the cut collapsed, killing many of the workers, he ended the project. But, according to one report, Sepúlveda had already found a number of gold objects and an emerald the size of a hen's egg.

The craziest attempt happened in 1911. A company owned by **Hartley Knowles** tunneled under the lake, creating a drain to empty it. It worked, but unfortunately, a thick layer of muck and slime lined the lake's bottom. Knowles found a few valuable items, but the hot sun soon baked the mud like cement, ending any chance to find more. The company gave up and plugged up the tunnel. The lake soon refilled.

Caribbean Sea

Pacific Ocean

●Lake Guatavita

Colombia was named after Italian explorer Christopher Columbus.

iPuzzle
Down the Drain

Can you get through the drainage
tunnel below Lake Guatavita
from START to END?

Start

End!

Jump to this
page **or** follow
the pipes.

LEAD ODOR is an anagram of EL DORADO.   CARTOON SQUID is an anagram of CONQUISTADOR.

1957 I've come to the newly built **Amundsen-Scott South Pole station** to see what life is like at the bottom of the earth. The answer: *brrr*!

Life Among the Polies

Antarctica is the only continent with no trees, permanent residents, traffic jams, war, liverwurst (that I've seen), school principals, or weather reports other than "cold today, cold tomorrow." What does it have? For the people who come here, it's a land of cooperation, learning, and peace. Yes, there is such a place on our planet! :-)

In 1959, 12 countries signed the **Antarctic Treaty**. Before that, seven of those countries had claimed parts of this frozen world. The treaty set those claims aside, neither recognizing nor rejecting them. It then banned military activity or nuclear-waste disposal and established that any research done here be shared. Antarctica officially became an oasis of peace and science. Another 38 countries later signed on.

Countries from every other continent have built research bases on Antarctica. But the coolest (in more ways than one) is the U.S.'s Amundsen-Scott South Pole station because it's at…the South Pole! The **Polies** (what the people here call themselves) have put up a barber-shop pole to mark it. There was once a volleyball net nearby, and each year, a **Christmas tree** built from scrap metal is set up.

These days, about 200 Polies live at the station in the summer. During the winter, the 50 or so who remain live in a world that's totally dark outside—the sun won't rise for half a year. They're also shut off from the world; the weather makes it impossible to leave or for others to visit. To kick things off each winter, the Polies show two horror movies, *The Shining*, about a family stranded alone for the winter in a vacant hotel, and *The Thing*, about an alien creature that terrorizes Antarctica.

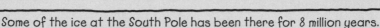

South Pole station, 1960

Sea spiders the size of dinner plates live in Antarctic waters.

Photos: South Pole station by the U.S. Navy. Barber pole by USAP, National Science Foundation

iPuzzle
Ice-udoku

meteorite

glove

penguin

snow

Draw pictures in the ice cubes so that
they follow the rules in the example.

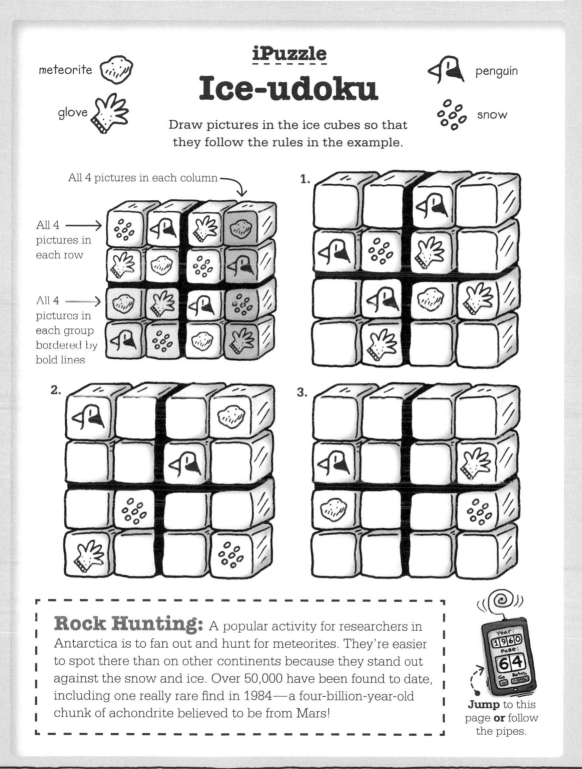

All 4 pictures in each column

All 4 → pictures in each row

All 4 → pictures in each group bordered by bold lines

1.

2.

3.

Rock Hunting: A popular activity for researchers in Antarctica is to fan out and hunt for meteorites. They're easier to spot there than on other continents because they stand out against the snow and ice. Over 50,000 have been found to date, including one really rare find in 1984—a four-billion-year-old chunk of achondrite believed to be from Mars!

year: 1960
Page: 64
Go Return

Jump to this page **or** follow the pipes.

Antarctica is bigger than the continental United States or Europe.

1976

I'm here on the shores of **Lake Victoria** in **Tanzania** to see **steel** being made by the **Haya people**, an art they nearly lost!

It's a Steel

charcoal and iron ore
(mined nearby)

chimney of termite mud

clay pipe

drum bellows

The Haya started making steel 2,000 years ago, about 19 centuries before **Europeans** developed a method as advanced. Their steelmaking furnaces were amazing, built using only natural materials that could be found around their village.

To make a furnace, the Haya dug a pit in the ground, lined it with the sandy mud of **termite mounds**, then used more termite mud to build a five-foot-tall **chimney** (1.5 m). A thick layer of charred **swamp grass** filled the furnace's pit, with a mix of **charcoal** and **iron** on top.

soil

termite mud lining

charred swamp grass

The furnace worked really well because of the incredible heat inside it—3275° F (1800° C). **Molten lava** is only about 2000° F! How did they do that? Eight men sat around the furnace pumping drum bellows (see next page) that fed air into the fire, making it burn hotter and hotter. Lumps of carbon steel were the result, which the Haya would fashion into spears, knives, and farming tools.

The Haya quit making steel in the early 20th century when **European mills** began producing lots of it cheaply. The Haya crafted their tools from recycled car parts instead and focused on growing **coffee** and **tea**. Their steelmaking method might have been lost forever if anthropologist **Peter Schmidt** hadn't visited the Haya village of **Nyungwe, Tanzania**, in 1976.

Schmidt found enough elders who had made steel as children—50 to 60 years before—and asked them to construct one of the steel furnaces. When the first four efforts failed, the elders consulted a diviner (spiritual leader).

He discovered the problem. An elder who hadn't been asked to help had hidden in the bushes and pointed his donkey at the furnace, sabotaging the project. (Really?) The fifth attempt (minus the bad-luck-donkey) was successful!

iPuzzle
Steel a Glance

In 1855, English inventor Henry Bessemer patented a process that allowed steel to be made cheaply on a large scale. Among other things, it made the car business possible. For this puzzle, find two parts that have been removed from each old car in comparison to the original.

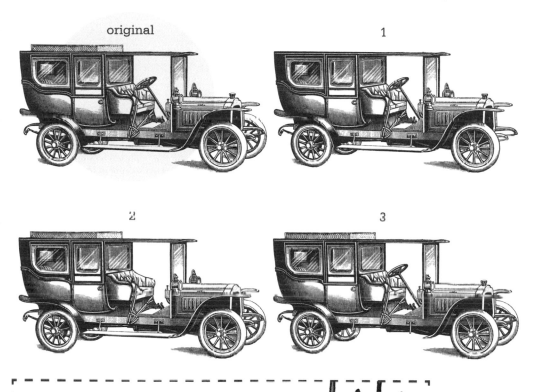

original   1

2   3

Drum Bellows: The Haya people used this device to pump air into their steelmaking furnaces. Sticks were pushed down on goatskin covers, forcing a blast of air into the fire.

pipe to furnace   air ◄------

Year: 2005
Page: 78
Go   Before

Jump to this page **or** follow the pipes.

The End

Congratulations, you've made it through 87 pages of history. And they said it couldn't be done! :-)

Did you notice something?

As promised on the front cover of this book, there hasn't been a single liverwurst sighting in these pages…well, except for the ones on pages 16, 47, 48, 71, 84, and 89. (Hey, nobody's perfect.)

But now that I've mentioned it…

…I'm a little hungry. So I'm cracking open a case of liverwurst (lab rats love the stuff) to munch on while you take the final quiz on the next page. The Four P's worked very hard to make sure every question in it deals with something that has appeared in this book.

Ridiculous Quiz

1. What does "acoustic" mean?
   - **a.** ___ one coustic
   - **b.** ___ it's what you hit a cue ball with on a pool table
   - **c.** ___ sound-related

2. Which U.S. President has the same first name as a *Sesame Street* character?
   - **a.** ___ Cookie Monster Monroe
   - **b.** ___ Big Bird Johnson
   - **c.** ___ Grover Cleveland

3. What is a mummy cat?
   - **a.** ___ the wife of a daddy cat
   - **b.** ___ a cat that's mum
   - **c.** ___ a sacred animal that ancient Egyptians buried

4. Which is a powdered-milk product that spells "milk" backward?
   - **a.** ___ REEB TOOR
   - **b.** ___ POP
   - **c.** ___ KLIM

5. What is this book's least favorite pink-colored sausage?
   - **a.** ___ an uncooked hot dog
   - **b.** ___ an uncooked breakfast link
   - **c.** ___ liverwurst, cooked or uncooked

6. Which word can be typed with the right hand only?
   - **a.** ___ RIGHT
   - **b.** ___ HAND
   - **c.** ___ ONLY

7. What are you going to do now that you've finished this book?
   - **a.** ___ read it again backward while standing on my head
   - **b.** ___ take an online I.Q. test to see if I'm any smarter
   - **c.** ___ run out and get the next iFlush book

Answers

9. It's Greek to Me

1. **ALPHA**BET
2. STU**PID**
3. U**PHI**LL
4. M**ETA**L
5. **TAU**GHT
6. PO**PSI**CLE
7. MI**NU**TE
8. MA**CHI**NE
9. A**MUS**ED
10. E**XIT**

Extra Credit:

11. CA**R HORN**
12. **THE TA**RGET

11. Polo Shirts

3 and 8 are identical.
1 is missing a white cuff on one sleeve.
2 is missing the top button.
4 is missing a pocket.
5 is missing a belt hole.
6 is missing a white cuff on one sleeve.
7 is missing part of the collar.

13. Wheels of Fortune

left: BECAUSE IT IS TOO TIRED (two-tired)
right: THE PAVEMENT

15. Pick Trick

ARITHMETIC, IDIOTIC and PANIC are not in the puzzle.

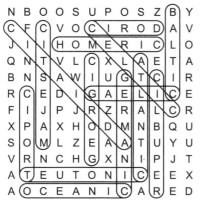

17. Lineup

The top right and lower left photos are identical.

The upper left photo is missing a man in front of the doorway.

In the lower right photo, the sign says EMPLOYED instead of UNEMPLOYED.

19. Add a BELL

1. TABLECLOTH
2. JELLYBEAN
3. EYEBALL
4. UMBRELLA
5. BELLIES
6. BALLET
7. BULLETIN
8. BASEBALL
9. LABEL

Extra Credit:

10. SYLLABLE
11. FLEXIBLE
12. BLOWHOLE

21. Party Time

Here are some words we found:

REPUBLICAN

1. LAB, LAP, LEA, LIE, LIP

2. BAIL, BALE, BANE, BARE, BARN, BEAN, BEAR, BEAU, BIER, BILE, BLIP, BLUE, BLUR, BRAN, BURL, BURN, BURP

3. PACER, PALER, PANEL, PANIC, PEARL, PECAN, PENAL, PERIL, PLACE, PLAIN, PLANE, PRICE, PRUNE

Extra credit: ALPINE, BURIAL, BURLAP, LINEAR, LINEUP, NEBULA, NEURAL, NUCLEI, PARCEL, PENCIL, PINCER, PLACER, PRANCE, PRINCE, PUBLIC, PUNIER, UNABLE, UNREAL, UNRIPE, URBANE

DEMOCRATIC

1. RAM, RAT, RED, RID, RIM, ROD, ROE, ROT

2. CAME, CARD, CARE, CART, CITE, COAT, CODA, CODE, COMA, COME, CORD, CORE, CRAM

3. TAMED, TAMER, TIMED, TIMER, TIRED, TRACE, TRADE, TREAD, TRIAD, TRICE, TRIED

Extra credit: ACCORD, ACETIC, ADMIRE, ADROIT, ARCTIC, ATOMIC, CARTED, COATED, CREDIT, DIRECT, DREAMT, EDITOR, METRIC, MITRED, REDACT, RIOTED, ROAMED, TIRADE, TRACED, TRIODE

23. Fence Defense

By adding fence sections at D, E, and G, a rabbit would be blocked from getting to the carrot.

25. Maya Match

1 + 3 = 4	SKY (already done)
10 - 9 = 1	SUN
2 x 3 = 6	SNAKE
9 ÷ 3 = 3	CRAB
2 + 3 = 5	HOUSE
11 - 4 = 7	BONE
2 x 4 = 8	BOOK
12 : 6 = 2	FIRE

27. Island-Hopping

Dwayne didn't visit MILL ROCK Island.

29. Cats!

1. CATHY
2. VACATION
3. EDUCATION
4. COPYCAT
5. LOCATE
6. CATERPILLAR
7. SCATTER
8. CATALOG
9. CERTIFICATE
10. CATCHER

31. Apollo 1-11

33. Pirate Search

iPuzzle Quickie: 1. C   2. A   3. B

35. Klim Cards

1. One silo is missing behind the barn. 2. "POWDERED MILK" has been moved on the roof. 3. There are extra windows on the front of the barn. 4. The orange bush is missing on the side of the barn. 5. Two children are missing. 6. The house on the right is missing. 7. There's much less white on the standing cow. 8. The lying-down cow has been moved to the right.

37. Treehouse Maze

39. A Dash of Salt

1. CORN, LAMB
2. NECK, CALF
3. CLUB, NAME
4. HAND, LUCK
5. CRAB, LION
6. SLAM, INCH
7. CAMP, ONLY
8. BEAN, COLD
9. CENT, TAIL

Extra credit:

10. CLAN
11. CANAL
12. VOLCANO
13. CLEAN
14. FALCON
15. ICELAND

41. Grover: Yes or No?

The false ones are 4 and 6.
President Taft reached a top weight of around 320 lbs. (145 kg). Cleveland never mentioned his views on walruses.

43. Current Events

45. Clan Scan

1. PONIES, DEEP FISH, HOT TOAD is not the actual clan name.
2. GREAT NAME BEARER is the clan name.
3. PIGEON HAWK is the clan name.
4. TWO TOP LADIES is not the clan name.
5. NEATER CABIN is not the clan name.
6. PAINTED TURTLE is the clan name.
7. LEG ROVER PAL is not the clan name.
8. STANDING ROCK is the clan name.

47. Lucky "13"

His name is Antonio de Padua María Severino López de Santa Anna y Pérez de Lebrón.

51. Windoku

53. Whazzat?

1. H
2. K
3. C
4. B
5. L
6. J
7. F
8. E
9. I
10. A
11. G
12. D

55. Double or Half?

Half: gold, house, toilet paper, bread
Double: gas, car, eggs, burger

57. Name Game

The answers in order from top to bottom are:

CENDRILLON, ASKEPOT, PELENÉ, TUHKIMO, KOPCIUSZEK, VENTAFOCS, PEPELJUGA, POPELKA, HIRUSHJA, CENICIENTA, KULKEDISI

The joke's answer:
SHE RAN AWAY FROM THE BALL.

59. Coded Jokes

A. 5, SNEAKERS
B. 4, W
C. 2, OUCH
D. 6, FIRECRACKERS
E. 3, JELLYFISH
F. 1, MARCH

61. Amusing Parks

1. REAL, 9
2. REAL, 8
3. FAKE, 12
4. REAL, 9
5. REAL, 7
6. FAKE, 11

63. Character Count

Both the BOAT character and SKY character appear 6 times.

ARMY: 3   BOAT: 6   ISLAND: 1
MAN: 4   RICE: 2   SEA: 5
SKY: 6   WAR: 8   YEAR: 7

Extra Credit: Since there are 9 different characters, that means there will be one of one character, two of a second, three of a third, and so on up to eight. The ninth character will then be a repeat of one of the other character's total.

So add up the counts for each character: $1 + 2 + 3 + 4 + 5 + 6 + 7 + 8 = 36$. Since there are 42 total characters, that means the 9th character must appear 6 times ($42 - 36 = 6$).

65. '60 Questions

1. G   3. E   5. A   7. C
2. D   4. H   6. B   8. F

67. Calendar Jokes

1. D   3. G   5. H   7. B   9. I
2. E   4. J   6. F   8. A   10. C

69. Wynne Win

Extra Credit: Change HARD to HARM and DOVE to MOVE (change D to M).

71. Scenes at a Picnic

The pictures should be numbered in this order:

5 7 1
3 6 8
2 9 4

73. Monopoly

1. TREES   2. OINK   3. BEAVER
4. SEEDS   5. HO HO HO   6. ZEBRA
7. MUMMY   8. JULY   9. EAST or WEST
10. PUMPKIN   11. BAT or CAT or RAT
12. *STAR WARS*   13. MILLION

Extra Credit—Here are some we found:
Left boys: Abe, Ace, Bart, Bert, Brad, Brett, Carter, Dave, Dexter, Drew, Edward, Ezra, Fred, Gerard, Greg, Red, Reed, Rex, Steve, Stewart, Tad, Ted, Wade, Ward, Wes
Right boys: Jim, Jimmy, Jin, John, Johnny, Julio, Kip, Lonny, Lou, Milo, Phil, Phillip
Left girls: Ava, Babe, Barbara, Barbra, Bea, Bette, Bev, Bree, Dee, Deedee, Eva, Eve, Freda, Grace, Greta, Sade, Teresa, Tess, Vera
Right girls: Holly, Jill, Jo, Jojo, Joni, Joy, Juno, Kiki, Kim, Kimiko, Kimmy, Kumiko, Lili, Lilly, Loni, Lulu, Lynn, Milly, Mimi, Molly, Nikki, Pippi, Polly, Poppy, Yoko

75. Volcano Search

77. Russian Around

1. D	4. A	7. B	9. I
2. J	5. E	8. C	10. F
3. H	6. G		

79. Size Them Up

1. *Spray* was 40 feet long.
2. *Victoria* was about 65 feet long.
3. *B&Q* is 75 feet long.
4. *Earthrace* is 78 feet long.
5. USS *Triton* is 447 feet long.
6. RMS *Laconia* was 601 feet long.

81. Tallest Tower

7 is the tallest at 11 blocks high.

5 is the shortest at 6 blocks high.

2 is 7 blocks high.
6 is 8 blocks high.
1, 3, 8, and 9 are all 9 blocks high.
4 is 10 blocks high.

83. Down the Drain

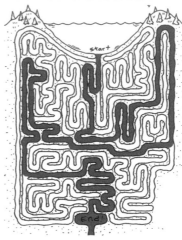

85. Ice-udoku

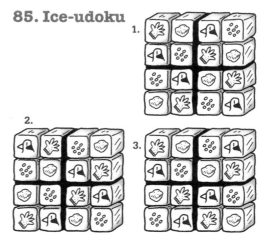

87. Steel a Glance

1 is missing a luggage carrier on its roof and one tire/wheel.

2 is missing its steering wheel and the radiator cap on the front of the hood.

3 is missing a lamp near the windshield and a running board between the tires.

89. Ridiculous Quiz

"C" is the correct answer for each, except for the last question. That's up to you!

The 1st book in the iFlush series—
iFlush: Swimming in Science

The 3rd and 4th iFlush books, coming in 2014:
Hunting for Heroes
Plunging into Mystery

Other outrageously cool For Kids Only! titles:

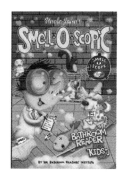

To order, contact:

Bathroom Readers' Press
P.O. Box 1117
Ashland, OR 97520
Phone: 888-488-4642
Fax: 541-482-6159

www.bathroomreader.com

iBonus
Make a Mayan Book

As promised on page 25, here are your top-secret iFlush instructions for making an accordion-style book.

1. Supplies

- one standard sheet of white copy paper
- drawing materials

This is all you need!

2. Fold over

Fold the sheet of paper in half the long way.

long side

3. Fold back

Fold it in half again, as shown.

4. Fold forward

Fold the front part in half toward you.

5. Fold away

Fold the back part in half away from you.

6. Ta da!

That's it! You have an accordion book.

7. Cover

Draw a cover. What's your book about?

RATS

8. Insides

Fill in the first 4 pages.

cover on back side

1 2 3 4

9. The end

Continue on the back 3 pages.

5 6 7 RATS